STAR WARS™

THE LIFE DAY COOKBOOK

STAR WARS™

THE LIFE DAY COOKBOOK

Official Holiday Recipes
From a Galaxy Far, Far Away

By Jenn Fujikawa and Marc Sumerak

Photography by Ted Thomas

INSIGHT
EDITIONS

SAN RAFAEL • LOS ANGELES • LONDON

CONTENTS

INTRODUCTION

It's me again. Your ol' pal, Cookie—or Chef Strono Tuggs, if you wanna get all formal about it—bringin' you a heapin' helpin' of gastronomical goodness specially designed for your Life Day revelries. Sure, I might not seem like the festive type on the surface, but this new batch of dishes is about way more than just me. Lemme explain . . .

Last time I sent out a collection of recipes from the edge of the galaxy, I thought I was makin' a definitive statement about who I was as a chef. I'd spanned the Core to the Outer Rim, masterin' the cuisines of countless cultures and spicin' 'em up with my own signature flair. And don't get me wrong, I still stand by every single one of those dishes. But as tasty as they may have been, some of 'em were missin' one important ingredient.

See, back when I was head chef at Maz Kanata's castle on Takodana, I found myself feedin' hundreds of rogues, rebels, pirates, and bounty hunters each day. And every single one of 'em had a story to tell. Whether they realized it or not, their tales are what shaped my recipes, inspirin' new flavors and techniques that would speak to their unique palates on a personal level.

When Maz's castle was destroyed by the First Order, I didn't just lose my kitchen . . . I lost that connection. And although the travels that followed may have led me to discoverin' all sorts of wild new ingredients and recipes, it was a pretty lonely journey. The direct link between chef and diner that had always pushed my meals to the next level had begun to fade without me even realizin' it. Wasn't 'til I finally stopped travelin' the galaxy and parked my food freighter for an extended stay on Batuu that I was reminded of how crucial a personal touch is, for each and every plate. A connection is the key to turnin' a meal into a memory.

Before I got to Batuu, I didn't know all that much about Life Day. It wasn't really somethin' we celebrated back on my homeworld, Artiod Minor. I knew about Life Day from Gormaanda's holovids, sure, but just the basics: It had somethin' to do with Wookiees and trees. And even though I was known to whip up my own special Wroshyr Tree Cake now and then to help a few lonely travelers mark the occasion, I'll be the first to admit that I never really got what it was all about. And it probably showed.

But the best chefs are the ones who are willin' to admit they still have a lot to learn, both in the kitchen and in the world outside. And the more stories I heard about Life Day from the constant stream of customers floodin' through Docking Bay 7, the more I realized how wrong I'd been about it all these years.

I mean, I was right about some things. Life Day started on the Wookiee homeworld of Kashyyyk to honor an ancient tree that they believed was the source of all life in the galaxy. The big lugs decorated their Tree of Life with glowin' orbs, got all fancied up in their finest robes, and sang festive songs. (Or at least I assume they were songs. Shyriiwook mostly sounds like a bunch of garbled growls to me.)

But as it turns out, the celebration wasn't limited only to folks of the tall and furry variety. See, deep at its core, Life Day wasn't really about Wookiees and trees at all— at least not entirely. It was about that one elusive ingredient I'd been searchin' for since I left Takodana: connection. With each other, with our traditions, and with the galaxy 'round us. So, it was only natural that the true message behind Life Day would spread from Coruscant to D'Qar, givin' folks a spark of hope, even in their darkest days. And it was the exact kinda spark I'd been searchin' for myself.

So as my new friends on Batuu eagerly hung their orbs and joined hands 'round the Spire, I made sure to listen close to the stories they'd carried with 'em from all across the galaxy. Stories of Life Day. Of Winter's Heart. Of Solstice Tide. No matter what they'd celebrated to mark the midwinter months back home, I wanted to learn more. Not only about what filled their bellies, but what filled their hearts.

Their stories are the inspiration for this new assortment of holiday-themed recipes. Unlike my first collection, this batch ain't meant to make some sort of grand proclamation about my culinary point of view. Because as much pride as I take preparin' every one of these dishes, like I said before, these ones aren't just about me.

> Life Day is about all of us.
> Get ready to dig in . . . again!
> **—COOKIE**

APPETIZERS AND SNACKS

In my opinion, there ain't no better time than the holidays to share what we love with those 'round us. For some folks, that means sharin' gifts. For most of my customers, it means sharin' stories. But for me, it means sharin' food. And the easiest way to get the most food to the most people is by servin' 'em a scrumptious spread of starters and snacks. Dependin' on the occasion, I've found that an amazin' assortment of apps like these often goes over even better than a massive multicourse meal!

When I'm caterin' an event 'round the midwinter months, I like to whip up a samplin' of small plates that highlights the seasonal traditions on a number of worlds. Sure, I may be throwin' a Life Day soirée, but there's no reason to leave out the folks who celebrate somethin' else. If one of these dishes can make 'em feel at home, even if they're light-years from it, then I've done my job.

In this section, you'll find some bite-size holiday favorites from across the galaxy that are easy to cook and sure to please. Don't matter how many batches of 'em you make—they're sure to vanish faster than an ice cube on Tatooine!

SHI-SHOK FRUIT BOWLS

There's somethin' special about goin' home for the holidays . . . but not all of us have got a place to go. See, I spent so many years in the kitchen of Maz's castle on Takodana that it became more of a home to me than Artiod Minor ever was. After the castle fell, I found myself roamin' the Outer Rim in my food freighter without any world to truly call my own. When I'm feelin' a little lost in this big ol' galaxy, I make myself a bowl of this simple fruit salad, which was always a favorite of Maz's most loyal patrons. I mix in whatever is in season—from jogans to shuura—but the sweetness of the shi-shok is what really brings it all together. The shi-shok happens to be native to Kashyyyk, which makes this one perfect for Life Day . . . or any day that you need a little taste of home.

2 dragon fruit (pink or white)

1 kiwi, peeled and diced

1 cup balled cantaloupe

½ cup raspberries

½ cup blueberries

¼ cup orange juice

1 teaspoon lime zest

> **PREP TIME:** 15 minutes
> **YIELD:** 4 servings
> **DIFFICULTY:** Easy

1. Halve the dragon fruit lengthwise. Use a melon baller to scoop out the flesh. Pat the shell dry with a paper towel. Set aside.

2. In a medium bowl, toss the balled dragon fruit, kiwi, cantaloupe, raspberries, and blueberries with the orange juice and lime zest. Spoon the fruit mixture into the dragon fruit shells to serve.

SPICED BOGWINGS

On most worlds, when the holidays roll 'round, the weather starts to get colder. When temperatures drop, I like to come up with creative culinary creations that can help turn up the heat. That's where these little fellas come in. Bogwings are reptavians native to Naboo, but their meat can be found for a decent price in just about any market across the Outer Rim. I like to coat their wings with a blend of mouthwaterin' spices procured by my friend Kat Saka, then bake 'em up in big batches. They make for a perfect party dish . . . but they should probably come with a warnin'. After all, a single bite of one of these makes my mouth feel like it's gone straight to Mustafar!

CHICKEN

3 pounds chicken wings

1½ tablespoons baking powder

1 teaspoon garlic powder

1 teaspoon onion powder

¼ teaspoon salt

¼ teaspoon black pepper

PREP TIME: 10 minutes

COOKING TIME: 50 minutes

YIELD: 6 servings

DIFFICULTY: Medium

SAUCE

¼ cup soy sauce

2 tablespoons packed light brown sugar

1 tablespoon gochujang

1 tablespoon rice vinegar

2 teaspoons gochugaru (Korean red pepper flakes)

1 teaspoon sesame oil

2 garlic cloves, minced

1. Preheat the oven to 400°F. Place a wire rack on a baking sheet.

2. **TO MAKE THE CHICKEN:** In a large bowl, toss the chicken wings with the baking powder, garlic powder, onion powder, salt, and black pepper. Place the seasoned wings on the prepped wire rack.

3. Bake the wings for 30 minutes, flip them, then bake for another 20 minutes, until the wings are golden brown.

4. **MAKE THE SAUCE:** While the wings cook, in a large bowl, stir together the soy sauce, brown sugar, gochujang, vinegar, gochugaru, sesame oil, and garlic.

5. When the wings are done, add them to the sauce and toss until coated.

6. Turn the oven to broil. Place the wings back on the wire rack and broil for 1 minute, until crispy. Serve hot.

BOLUS NUTS

Back in the day, when Jedha was still in one piece, pilgrims used to flock to the desert moon's Holy City every year to celebrate somethin' called Reflection Day. Most of 'em journeyed all that way just to stare into a fancy kyber mirror in hopes that the Force would reveal their future . . . or some philosophical nonsense like that. But the truly enlightened travelers? We came to Jedha early for the street food! Stalls were set up all over the city on Reflection Eve, with vendors peddlin' festive cuisine from across the galaxy. I can still smell the whole roast turniks spinnin' on their spits! But of all the portable provisions to partake of, none were quite as delightful as the sweet, sticky bolus nuts. On Jedha, they were served on sticks, but I prefer these crunchy little treats by the bowlful. Get your mitts on some of these, and I guarantee your future will be bright!

1 large egg white

2 cups almonds

1 teaspoon vanilla extract

¾ cup packed light brown sugar

1 teaspoon ground cinnamon

¼ teaspoon ground nutmeg

¼ teaspoon salt

PREP TIME: 5 minutes

COOKING TIME: 1 hour

YIELD: 12 servings

DIFFICULTY: Easy

1. Preheat the oven to 250°F. Prep a baking sheet with parchment paper.

2. In a large bowl, using a hand mixer, whip the egg white until frothy, 1 to 2 minutes. Stir in the almonds and vanilla, tossing to coat.

3. In a large sealable bag, combine the brown sugar, cinnamon, nutmeg, and salt. Add the almonds and shake until coated.

4. Spread the nuts evenly on the prepped baking sheet. Bake for 1 hour, stirring every 15 minutes, until the sugar mixture has melted. Let cool completely, then serve.

SAAVA SNACKS

The forests of Kashyyyk are dense with lush vegetation, which makes the Wookiees pretty happy, what with their love of all things natural. Their woodlands are teemin' with fresh, organic ingredients that are ideal for just about any meal. But some of the native flora on that wild Wookiee world are just as likely to snack on you as you are to snack on 'em. Saava is one of those pesky plants—a carnivorous parasite of sorts that latches on to its prey and slowly devours it over time. On the plus side, the saava also happens to produce an absolutely delectable fruit that is almost worth the risk it takes to harvest one. If you can avoid gettin' all tangled up in a saava's vines, you'll find yourself with a sweet snack that everyone will savor. And if you can't? Well, at least the saava gets to eat . . .

4 figs, quartered

2 tablespoons extra-virgin olive oil

½ teaspoon salt

¼ teaspoon black pepper

¾ cup feta cheese

⅓ cup toasted pecans, chopped

⅓ cup honey

PREP TIME: 5 minutes

COOKING TIME: 15 minutes

YIELD: 16 servings

DIFFICULTY: Easy

1. Preheat the oven to 425°F. Prep a baking sheet with parchment paper.

2. In a large bowl, lightly toss the figs with the olive oil, salt, and black pepper. Place the seasoned figs on the prepped baking sheet. Evenly divide the feta cheese among each fig.

3. Bake for 10 to 12 minutes, until the cheese is melted and bubbly. Sprinkle with the pecans and drizzle with the honey to serve.

MILLAFLOWER TOAST

As a chef, it ain't just my job to make food taste good. If I want my customers to pop somethin' new into one of their mouth holes, I gotta make it look and smell good, too. Thanks to the millaflower, that part of my job is easy. These fragrant edible blossoms are native to Naboo and class up just about any dish, turnin' a simple snack into somethin' elegant and exquisite. Don't believe me? Just toast up a slice of bread, spread on some soft moof milk cheese, top it with some local fruit or veg, and then add on a few of these beautiful blooms! I enjoy this tasty treat year-round, but it's become a huge hit 'round Life Day, since the vibrant red hues seem to remind folks of the fancy robes that Wookiees wear durin' their sacred celebration.

1 cup ricotta cheese

1 tablespoon lemon zest

6 ciabatta slices, lightly toasted

¾ cup halved cherry tomatoes

¾ cup sliced strawberries

2 teaspoons extra-virgin olive oil

½ teaspoon salt

¼ teaspoon black pepper

2 tablespoons balsamic vinegar

1 tablespoon honey

¼ cup edible flowers, such as garden pansies,
cornflowers, nasturtiums,
or marigolds, for garnish

PREP TIME: 5 minutes

YIELD: 6 servings

DIFFICULTY: Easy

1. In a small bowl, stir together the ricotta and lemon zest. Spread the mixture on the ciabatta slices, then set aside.

2. In a medium bowl, toss the tomatoes and strawberries with the olive oil. Spoon the mixture on top of the ricotta, then season with the salt and black pepper.

3. Drizzle the vinegar on top, followed by the honey. Garnish with the edible flowers to serve.

KEBROOT PARCELS

Been a long time since Alderaan was destroyed by the Death Star. But even though there may not be much left of the planet itself these days, stories of its holiday celebration, Winter's Heart, have managed to live on. From what I've heard, the Alderaanians used to throw quite a feast every year, with a roast kulkan as the centerpiece. They didn't skimp on the fixins neither, boilin' up a variety of veg—includin' kebroot tubers—to complement the main course. Naturally, folks who were off-planet when Alderaan was blown up find themselves pretty desperate for some culinary comfort whenever midwinter rolls 'round. Hopefully, these mouthwaterin' Kebroot Parcels manage to capture the flavor of Winter's Heart for anyone who still remembers it.

FILLING

2 medium sweet potatoes, scrubbed

18 dried corn husks

One 14.5-ounce can black beans, drained

½ cup sweet corn

2 tablespoons chopped roasted green chiles

½ teaspoon chili powder

½ teaspoon ground cumin

½ teaspoon salt

¼ teaspoon garlic powder

⅛ teaspoon black pepper

MASA

2 cups masa harina

1 teaspoon salt

1 teaspoon baking powder

1 cup vegetable broth, warmed

½ cup extra-virgin olive oil

Salsa verde, for serving

PREP TIME: 1 hour

COOKING TIME: 2 hours

YIELD: 18 servings

DIFFICULTY: Hard

1. Preheat the oven to 375°F and prep a baking sheet with parchment paper.

2. **TO MAKE THE FILLING:** Use a fork to prick the sweet potatoes. Place them on the prepped baking sheet and bake for 1 hour, until tender. Let the potatoes cool slightly, then peel and discard the skin. Mash with a fork until smooth. Set aside.

3. Meanwhile, soak the corn husks in warm water for 45 minutes. Remove them from the water and pat dry.

4. In a medium saucepan over medium-low heat, combine the black beans, corn, green chiles, chili powder, cumin, salt, garlic powder, and black pepper. Simmer for 5 to 7 minutes, until fragrant and warmed through. Set aside.

5. **TO MAKE THE MASA:** In a large bowl whisk together the masa harina, salt, and baking powder. Add the broth and olive oil a little at a time. Mix for 5 minutes, until paste-like.

6. Place a corn husk on a clean surface, narrow end facing away from you. Spread 3 tablespoons of masa on the corn husk. Add 1 tablespoon of mashed sweet potatoes and 1 tablespoon of bean mixture to the center. To close, fold in the left side, then the right, then fold the end of the husk upward toward the top end. Tie with a thin piece of corn husk, set aside, and continue with the rest of the masa and filling.

7. Add a steamer basket to a large pot, then fill the pot with water just up to the basket (but not touching). Bring to a simmer over medium-high heat, then reduce the heat to low. Add the tamales standing upright. Cover and steam for 1 hour, adding more water if necessary, until the tamales are easily removed off the husk. Serve with salsa verde.

YALBEC STINGERS

The holidays are the perfect time to splurge a little. Servin' up a dish made from a fancy, expensive ingredient is an easy way to remind folks just how much an occasion really means. Lucky for me, my pal Dok-Ondar on Batuu knows his stuff when it comes to rare delicacies. Last Life Day, he managed to score me the stinger of an insect queen from Yalbec Prime. And because I knew how hard it was for him to acquire, that spectacular spike was suddenly more than just sweet and sumptuous: It was special. Of course, most of us can't afford an actual Yalbec stinger, so I whipped up this recipe in hopes of capturin' the same exquisite flavors at a fraction of the cost. Sure, they may not be the real deal, but this batch of stingers is anythin' but bad!

4 ounces cream cheese, softened

4 ounces sour cream

1 garlic clove, minced

1 tablespoon chopped fresh parsley

1 teaspoon chopped fresh chives

1 teaspoon chopped fresh basil

1 teaspoon chopped fresh thyme

¼ teaspoon salt

⅛ teaspoon black pepper

14 mini bell peppers, halved and seeded

PREP TIME: 5 minutes

YIELD: 4 servings

DIFFICULTY: Easy

1. In a small bowl, stir together the cream cheese, sour cream, garlic, parsley, chives, basil, thyme, salt, and black pepper.

2. Pipe the filling into the bell peppers. Refrigerate until ready to serve.

CRAB PUFFS

Awhile back, I found myself stranded at a port on the aquatic world of Mon Cala while gettin' some much-needed maintenance on my trusty food freighter. While I was waitin' for the repairs, I ventured into a nearby waterin' hole to get myself a bit more familiar with the local cuisine. After a few hours tradin' recipes with the joint's Mon Calamari chef, he told me about a special crab-stuffed puff that his people made to celebrate Life Day.

The strange secret to this nautical nibble? The tiny crabs inside the puff were still alive! Personally, I tend to prefer a tasty bite that doesn't bite back, so I made my own deep-fried variation. This one captures the flavors of the Mon Cala original but without the risk of any claws up in your craw.

1 pound lump crabmeat

1 garlic clove, minced

1 large egg, lightly beaten

2 tablespoons mayonnaise

2 tablespoons grated Parmesan cheese

1 teaspoon lemon juice

½ teaspoon onion powder

½ teaspoon paprika

½ teaspoon salt

¼ teaspoon black pepper

1 cup panko bread crumbs

2 cups vegetable oil, for frying

1 tablespoon minced fresh parsley

PREP TIME: 5 minutes

COOKING TIME: 15 minutes

YIELD: 12 servings

DIFFICULTY: Medium

1. In a large bowl, combine the crabmeat, garlic, egg, mayonnaise, Parmesan cheese, lemon juice, onion powder, paprika, salt, and black pepper. Fold the mixture together until just combined. Scoop and roll the mixture into 1-inch balls. Place the bread crumbs in a shallow dish, then roll each ball in the bread crumbs. Set aside.

2. In a Dutch oven over medium-high heat, heat the vegetable oil to 350°F. Working in batches to avoid overcrowding, add the balls and fry for about 3 minutes, or until golden brown. Let the balls drain on a wire rack, then sprinkle with the parsley to serve.

SOLSTICE VEGISPHERES

Visit just about any world in the galaxy, and you're bound to find some variation of the meatball in that culture's culinary catalog. Doesn't matter if it's made of nerf, gornt, or even a plant-based mixture, the basic idea behind 'em is still the same: Shape some hearty ingredients into tiny spheres, sauté 'em in a savory sauce, and enjoy! Since Life Day is all about findin' connection, it makes perfect sense to share a food that every species can relate to. My spin on this classic leaves the "meat" outta the "meatball" to keep things all-inclusive while still feelin' warm, comfortin', and familiar, no matter what system you call home. Of course, you're not required to celebrate any specific midwinter holiday in order to enjoy these meatless morsels. But there's a pretty good chance they'll bring you good cheer either way.

VEGISPHERES

2 pieces white bread, torn

⅓ cup soy milk

4 tablespoons olive oil, divided

½ cup minced onion

1 stalk celery, minced

1 medium carrot, finely grated

½ cup minced white mushrooms

One 15-ounce can garbanzo beans

½ teaspoon ground allspice

½ teaspoon cardamom

½ teaspoon salt

¼ teaspoon ground nutmeg

¼ teaspoon black pepper

GRAVY

2 tablespoons coconut oil

2 tablespoons all-purpose flour

1¾ cups vegetable broth

¼ cup full-fat coconut cream

½ teaspoon salt

¼ teaspoon black pepper

1 teaspoon minced fresh parsley, for garnishing

PREP TIME: 30 minutes

COOKING TIME: 35 minutes

YIELD: 6 servings

DIFFICULTY: Medium

1. **TO MAKE THE VEGISPHERES:** In a small bowl, soak the bread pieces in the soy milk. Set aside.

2. In a skillet over medium-high heat, heat 2 tablespoons of the olive oil and cook the onions, celery, carrots, and mushrooms until soft, 8 to 10 minutes. Let cool slightly.

3. In a large bowl use an immersion blender to mash the garbanzo beans into a smooth paste. Add the soaked bread, cooked vegetable mixture, allspice, cardamom, salt, nutmeg, and pepper. Stir until just combined. Form 16 balls.

4. In a skillet, heat the remaining olive oil and cook balls until browned on all sides, about 5 minutes. Transfer to a plate and cover with foil to keep warm.

5. **TO MAKE THE GRAVY:** To the same skillet over medium heat, add the coconut oil and flour and whisk until brown, 1 to 2 minutes. Whisk in vegetable broth and simmer until thick, 4 to 5 minutes. Stir in the coconut cream, and season with salt and pepper.

6. Add the balls back into the skillet; and simmer for another 5 minutes until warmed through. Garnish with parsley to serve.

PICKLED MYNOCK

Before I got to Batuu, I always assumed that mynock weren't good for much . . . 'cept for chewin' through your ship's cables and leavin' you stranded in the depths of space, of course.

But a trip to Oga's Cantina changed my tune about these power-hungry pests. See, Oga's bartenders keep a small assortment of pickled beasts on the shelf—includin' a worrt, a swamp slug, and even a mynock—to boost their legendary libations into hyperspace. When I managed to convince one of 'em to crack open the tank and lemme sample a piece of the mynock, I was blown away by the flavor.

Now, instead of cursin' those beastly things for drainin' my ship dry, I'm proudly servin' pickled mynock to any partygoer eager to fuel up!

1 pound large shrimp, tail on, peeled, and deveined

½ cup rice wine vinegar

½ cup lemon juice

½ cup extra-virgin olive oil

2 tablespoons capers with brine

1 teaspoon packed light brown sugar

1 teaspoon salt

½ teaspoon red pepper flakes

¼ teaspoon whole black peppercorns

¼ teaspoon celery seed

¼ cup coarsely chopped fresh dill

1 medium shallot, sliced lengthwise

2 whole garlic cloves, peeled

1 medium lemon, thinly sliced

PREP TIME: 5 minutes, plus overnight to pickle

COOKING TIME: 5 minutes

YIELD: 4 servings

DIFFICULTY: Easy

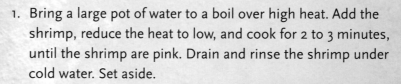

1. Bring a large pot of water to a boil over high heat. Add the shrimp, reduce the heat to low, and cook for 2 to 3 minutes, until the shrimp are pink. Drain and rinse the shrimp under cold water. Set aside.

2. In a large bowl, stir together the vinegar, lemon juice, olive oil, capers, brown sugar, salt, red pepper flakes, peppercorns, celery seed, dill, shallot, and garlic.

3. In a clean sealable quart jar, combine the shrimp and lemon slices. Pour in the vinegar mixture and seal the jar. Refrigerate overnight before serving. Keeps in the refrigerator for one week.

Side Dishes

A feast ain't much of a feast if it don't have all the fixins, no matter what day you serve it on. A big slab of roasted meat may look impressive on your table, but even a falumpaset can't carry a holiday meal all on its own. Every chef knows that it's essential to have an array of carefully planned accompaniments to balance out the flavors and offer some much-needed variation to the meal.

When it comes to side dishes, I try to find ingredients that complement the main course while addin' somethin' new and unexpected to the plate. Sometimes it's a blast of flavor from a tart fruit. Other times it's a splash of color from a vibrant veg. But it's always somethin' that brings out the best in every bite.

Sides can also go a long way toward makin' a meal feel even more authentic. In the case of Life Day, that means goin' back to basics and focusin' on classic Kashyyykian cuisine. After all, can a feast really be considered traditional if shi-shok or orga root ain't on the menu? Accordin' to most Wookiees I know, absolutely not.

I know that cookin' up all of these extra components seems like a lotta labor for little reward. But if you're willin' to put in the work and take things from meat to meal, I promise it'll make all the difference.

Plicated Orga Root

One of the first things I learned as a chef was to respect my ingredients. In most cases, that just means bringin' out the very best in every dish to maximize each component's natural flavor. But in the case of Kashyyyk's orga root, respect has gotta go a lot further than that. Though it ain't carnivorous like its fellow native plant the saava, the orga still has aggressive defense mechanisms to protect itself from potential harm. Its strong, sharp vines and acid pods are more than enough to fend off even the strongest of Wookiees. But as it turns out, an orga plant will offer its roots freely to folks who treat 'em with just the right amount of admiration. Orga may grow way down on Kashyyyk's forest floor, but they've earned a reverence from the planet's population that has elevated 'em to nearly sacred status.

2 medium russet potatoes, scrubbed

2 medium sweet potatoes, scrubbed

6 tablespoons unsalted butter, melted

¼ cup avocado oil

1 garlic clove, minced

2 tablespoons grated Parmesan cheese

½ teaspoon onion powder

½ teaspoon salt

¼ teaspoon paprika

¼ teaspoon black pepper

1 tablespoon minced fresh parsley

PREP TIME: 15 minutes

COOKING TIME: 1 hour

YIELD: 4 servings

DIFFICULTY: Medium

1. Preheat the oven to 425°F. Prep a baking sheet with parchment paper greased with nonstick spray.

2. Slice the sweet potatoes crosswise into ⅛-inch slices, stopping two-thirds of the way down before slicing all the way through. Place the potatoes on the prepped baking sheet.

3. In a small bowl, stir together the butter, avocado oil, garlic, Parmesan cheese, onion powder, salt, paprika, and black pepper. Use a pastry brush to brush the butter mixture on the sliced potatoes, getting in between the slices.

4. Bake for 50 to 60 minutes, until tender. Sprinkle with the parsley to serve.

SPINE TREE SPEARS

For some reason, a bunch of the galaxy's midwinter holidays seem to involve trees. Although the wroshyr tree on Kashyyyk may be the galaxy's most famous festive flora— what with it bein' the centerpiece of Life Day and all—it certainly ain't alone. For instance, durin' Solstice Tide, folks on Coruscant used to transport vecari trees all the way from Seylott, coverin' 'em with glow-globes and linin' 'em up and down Republic Avenue. I guess no matter where you live, seein' a bit of green survivin' through the sometimes harsh white of winter can be a pretty powerful symbol of hope. And because I'm a firm believer that what's on our plate should be a reflection of what's in our heart, I found this great recipe on Lothal that uses the spears of the spine tree to honor the season's arboreal aesthetic.

4 cups Romanesco cauliflower florets

2 tablespoons extra-virgin olive oil

1 tablespoon lemon zest

2 garlic cloves, minced

½ teaspoon salt

¼ teaspoon black pepper

PREP TIME: 10 minutes

COOKING TIME: 20 minutes

YIELD: 4 servings

DIFFICULTY: Easy

1. Preheat the oven to 425°F.

2. In a large bowl, toss together the Romanesco, olive oil, lemon zest, garlic, salt, and black pepper. Spread the mixture out on a baking sheet.

3. Roast for 15 to 17 minutes, until crispy and lightly charred. Serve warm.

Wroshyr Bramble

Life Day's origins can be found in Wookiee legends about the Tree of Life, the mythical wroshyr tree from which all life supposedly sprung. Since wroshyr trees are so important to the heart of the holiday, it felt only natural to find a way to incorporate 'em into this collection. But that's where things got tricky. See, it's common knowledge that wroshyr sap can be turned into a syrup, a glaze, or even a beverage. But the rest of the tree ain't exactly renowned for bein' edible. It took a lotta diggin'—literally—but I eventually found a part of the wroshyr that had the taste I was lookin' for. The tips of the wroshyr's root system add just the right amount of flavor and crunch to this classic veg casserole. It's like they always say: When it comes to holidays, it's always important to remember your roots!

Two 14.5-ounce cans French cut green beans, drained

One 10.75-ounce can condensed cream of mushroom soup

½ cup shredded Cheddar cheese

½ teaspoon garlic powder

¼ teaspoon paprika

¼ teaspoon black pepper

1½ cups store-bought crispy fried onions, divided

PREP TIME: 10 minutes

COOKING TIME: 40 minutes

YIELD: 6 servings

DIFFICULTY: Easy

1. Preheat the oven to 350°F. Prep an 8-by-8-inch baking dish with nonstick spray.

2. In a large bowl, stir together the green beans, soup, Cheddar cheese, garlic powder, paprika, black pepper, and half of the fried onions. Transfer the mixture to the prepped dish. Bake for 30 minutes, until bubbly.

3. Add the remaining half of fried onions on top. Return the dish to the oven and bake another 5 to 7 minutes, until the onions brown. Serve warm.

WAWAATT SPROUTS

As more cultures continue to embrace the message of Life Day, folks on distant worlds are startin' new traditions that capture the spirit of the occasion in their own special ways. But you might be surprised to learn that even the Wookiees themselves have variations in their sacred celebration, dependin' on what part of Kashyyyk they happen to inhabit.

In other words, you're not gonna get the same Life Day meal on Mount Arayakyak as you would in tree cities like Awrathakka or Rwookrrorro. For those who dwell on the Wawaatt Archipelago—a lush collection of islands home to the planet's capital, Kachirho—these flavorful sprouts have become an essential part of the holiday feast there.

Just one taste of their nutty sweetness and you'll be likely to add 'em on to your list of Life Day traditions, too!

SPROUTS

12 ounces Brussels sprouts

1 tablespoon extra-virgin olive oil

¼ teaspoon black pepper

¼ teaspoon salt

⅓ cup dried cranberries

DRESSING

1 tablespoon balsamic vinegar

1 tablespoon packed light brown sugar

2 teaspoons maple syrup

PREP TIME: 10 minutes

COOKING TIME: 30 minutes

YIELD: 10 servings

DIFFICULTY: Easy

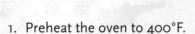

1. Preheat the oven to 400°F.

2. **TO MAKE THE SPROUTS:** Trim and halve the Brussels sprouts.
    On a baking sheet, toss the sprouts with the olive oil, salt,
    and black pepper. Roast for 30 minutes, until browned.

3. In a large bowl, toss together the sprouts and cranberries.

4. **TO MAKE THE DRESSING:** Meanwhile, in a small bowl, whisk
    together the vinegar, brown sugar, and maple syrup.

5. Pour the dressing over the sprouts and cranberries to serve.

RORKID BREAD

If one of my famous soups or stews finds their way onto the menu for your midwinter festivities, you can bet that your guests won't wanna leave a single bite of broth behind at the bottom of the bowl. And although a spoon usually gets the job done just fine, there's nothin' quite like soakin' up those last few drops with a nice hunk of seasoned bread. Truth be told, bakin' hasn't always been my strong suit, but I get by well enough. And in the case of this pungent, herby knot of Endorian rorkid bread, I've got the Ewoks to thank for a recipe that I ain't managed to mess up yet. This winter roll is traditionally served alongside bowls of Kublag Curry (page 67), but it'd be equally good alongside anythin' else you happen to be ladlin' out.

DOUGH

3 cups all-purpose flour

1½ teaspoons instant dry yeast

1 teaspoon salt

½ teaspoon garlic powder

¼ teaspoon onion powder

1 cup warm water (110°F)

1 tablespoon extra-virgin olive oil, plus more for greasing

TOPPING

6 tablespoons unsalted butter, melted

4 garlic cloves, minced

½ teaspoon dried basil

½ teaspoon dried oregano

¼ teaspoon salt

1 tablespoon matcha powder

PREP TIME: 20 minutes, plus 1 hour 30 minutes to rise

COOKING TIME: 25 minutes

YIELD: 14 servings

DIFFICULTY: Medium

Continued on next page . . .

1. **TO MAKE THE DOUGH:** In the bowl of an electric mixer fitted with a dough hook, mix together the flour, yeast, salt, garlic powder, and onion powder. Make a well in the center of the flour mixture, then stir in the water and olive oil, mixing for 5 minutes, until combined and formed into a ball.

2. Grease a large bowl with olive oil and place the dough in the bowl. Cover and let rise in a warm place for 1 hour, until doubled in size. Prep a baking sheet with parchment paper.

3. Punch the dough down and knead on a floured surface for 2 to 3 minutes, until stretchy. Separate the dough into 14 equal pieces. Roll out the pieces into ropes and fold them over into knots, tucking the ends underneath. Place the knots on the prepped baking sheet, cover, and let rise for 30 minutes.

4. Preheat the oven to 375°F.

5. **TO MAKE THE TOPPING:** In a small bowl, stir together the butter, garlic, basil, oregano, and salt.

6. Brush half of the butter mixture on the knots, then bake for 25 minutes, until lightly browned. Brush the knots with the remaining butter mixture. Dust with the matcha powder to serve.

TABA LEAF SALAD

Sometimes the holidays feel like an excuse to overindulge in ways you'd never imagine durin' the rest of the year. With so many glorious smells and beautiful spreads, it can be hard to resist packin' your plate so full that you'd need a loadlifter droid to carry it back to your seat at the table. That's why I always try to throw in a few healthier options, like this one, to the mix. Not only does this green salad bring a pop of color to the plate, it's got a fruity dressin' that adds a touch of festive flavor. It's also pretty versatile, workin' equally well as an openin' course, a side dish, or a post-meal palate cleanser. But if you ain't got room left in your belly for salad on the big day, maybe consider makin' this the day after to help you recover!

DRESSING

½ cup drained lychee

1 medium shallot, quartered

⅓ cup champagne vinegar

1 tablespoon Dijon mustard

1 tablespoon honey

1 teaspoon salt

½ teaspoon black pepper

½ cup extra-virgin olive oil

SALAD

5 ounces baby spinach

1 cup drained lychee

1 cup cubed avocado

1 cup sliced cucumber

½ cup blueberries

½ cup sliced red onion

PREP TIME: 20 minutes

YIELD: 6 servings

DIFFICULTY: Easy

1. **TO MAKE THE DRESSING:** In a blender, combine the lychee, shallot, vinegar, mustard, honey, salt, and black pepper. As it blends, pour in a steady stream of the olive oil until the dressing comes together. Keep in the refrigerator until ready to use.

2. **TO MAKE THE SALAD:** In a large bowl, combine the spinach, lychee, avocado, cucumber, blueberries, and onion.

3. Add the dressing to the salad and toss to serve.

Brub Berry Sauce

There are all kinds of sauces that you can add to a meal to boost its flavors to new heights. Over the years, I've tried out just about every type of gravy and dressin' you can imagine. And although most of 'em were designed to complement a specific dish, there are a few special sauces that can stand entirely on their own. One of those happens to be this fruity compote made from the winter berries of the Endorian brub-brub bush. It's sweet and tart at the same time, brightenin' your palate—and hopefully your day—with every bite. Brub berry sauce is a great counterpart to main courses like Engine Roasted Tip-Yip (page 69) or Glazed Kod'yok (page 54), but there's a solid chance you'll be just as glad to gobble up a bowl of this stuff on its own.

1 pint fresh blueberries

¼ cup packed light brown sugar

¼ cup orange juice

1 tablespoon maple syrup

½ teaspoon ground cinnamon

¼ teaspoon ground nutmeg

¼ teaspoon salt

⅛ teaspoon ground cloves

PREP TIME: 5 minutes

COOKING TIME: 10 minutes

YIELD: 8 servings

DIFFICULTY: Easy

1. In a small saucepan over low heat, combine the blueberries, brown sugar, orange juice, maple syrup, cinnamon, nutmeg, salt, and cloves. Use a masher to smash half of the blueberries.

2. Simmer for 10 minutes, stirring every few minutes, until thickened. Store in an airtight container in the refrigerator for up to one week.

Cirilian Noodle Salad

Way out near the edge of Wild Space on the planet Castilon, there used to be a refuelin' platform called the *Colossus* with a tavern run by a Gilliand named Z'Vk'Thkrkza. Known to her patrons as Aunt Z, she had a personality as bold as her signature Cirilian sour paste—which didn't sit too well with the First Order when they seized control of the platform. Taken into custody just for speakin' her mind, Aunt Z managed to break free and lead a group of dissidents to safety on Takodana. That's where she crossed paths with yours truly. We not only shared our recipes, but we shared an instant connection too. Sadly, her stay ended up bein' far too short for my tastes. No clue where she is now, but I'd trade a Life Day miracle or two to see that ol' gal again. As good as this Cirilian Noodle Salad is, it ain't quite the same if she's not here to share it with me.

DRESSING

¼ cup sweet chili sauce

2 tablespoons rice vinegar

2 teaspoons soy sauce

1 teaspoon sesame oil

1 garlic clove, minced

⅛ teaspoon black pepper

NOODLES

8 cups water

½ head red cabbage, chopped

6 ounces rice noodles

SALAD

4 cups shredded cabbage

2 medium carrots, peeled and julienned

1 cup snap peas, halved

1 scallion, white and green parts diced

1 teaspoon sesame seeds

1 lime, cut into wedges

PREP TIME: 20 minutes

COOKING TIME: 5 minutes

YIELD: 6 servings

DIFFICULTY: Medium

1. **TO MAKE THE DRESSING:** In a medium bowl, whisk together the chili sauce, vinegar, soy sauce, sesame oil, garlic, and black pepper. Set aside.

2. **TO MAKE THE NOODLES:** In a large pot over high heat, combine the water and cabbage. Bring to a boil, then scoop out and discard the cabbage. Add the rice noodles and boil for 2 to 3 minutes, until softened. Drain and set aside.

3. **TO MAKE THE SALAD:** In a serving bowl, toss the cabbage, carrots, and snap peas. Add the cooked noodles, scallion, and sesame seeds, tossing to combine.

4. Add dressing to serve. Serve with the lime wedges and squeeze them over the salad to change the noodle color.

Gloomroot Pancakes

Just the mention of Life Day usually conjures up images of light and happiness. So, it's a bit surprisin' that a number of the most popular dishes shared on this special day stem from Kashyyyk's darkest forests. The Shadowlands may be home to countless perils, includin' slyyygs, wyyyschokk, and jaw plants, but they also happen to be where some of the planet's tastiest ingredients grow. One of those is the gloomroot, a sweet and versatile tuber that grows not too far from Origin Lake. If you shred 'em up, gloomroots make the foundation of a lovely pancake. I like to add in some other root veg to enhance the sweetness and add a bit of color. Hard to believe that someplace so dismal could bring somethin' this vibrant to the table!

3 large russet potatoes, peeled

2 medium rainbow carrots, peeled

½ medium onion

1 large egg

3 tablespoons matzo meal

1 tablespoon all-purpose flour

1 teaspoon salt

⅛ teaspoon black pepper

½ cup vegetable oil

½ cup applesauce, for serving

½ cup sour cream, for serving

PREP TIME: 30 minutes

COOKING TIME: 15 minutes

YIELD: 12 servings

DIFFICULTY: Medium

1. Using the coarse side of a box grater, grate the potatoes, carrots, and onion. Use a cheesecloth to squeeze out all of the water from the grated vegetables.

2. Place the grated vegetables in a large bowl. Add the egg, matzo meal, flour, salt, and black pepper, stirring to combine.

3. In a large skillet over medium-high heat, heat the vegetable oil until it shimmers. While the oil warms, flatten ¼-cup portions of potato mixture into patties. Working in batches if necessary, add the patties to the oil and fry on each side for 3 to 4 minutes, until golden brown. Transfer the patties to a wire rack to drain.

4. Serve warm with the applesauce and sour cream.

Main Courses

When you spend your days cookin' from a food freighter, you find yourself feedin' an endless stream of hungry customers at every port you visit. That means you gotta focus on techniques that maximize flavor while keepin' cookin' time to a minimum. Over the years, I've mastered fast and flavorful cuisine, but every now and then, I like to slow things down and make a fancy meal usin' time-tested techniques. Lucky for me, most folks prefer their Life Day meals with an extra dash of tradition.

When appetizers alone just don't feel special enough, one of these main courses can serve as the centerpiece for just about any holiday banquet. From exotic meats to hearty stews, they're all designed to showcase the flavors of the midwinter months while appealin' to diverse and discernin' palates.

Servin' just one of these traditional dishes on your special day should be more than enough to impress almost any guest. But if you wanna go the extra parsec, make a few options to help out folks with dietary needs different from your own.

Whatever you choose to cook, be sure to respect the meal as much as you do the day it's served on. For me, that means actually takin' my time to enjoy preparin' it. If that's somethin' you just can't manage, then promise me you'll at least try to enjoy eatin' it!

TRASK CHOWDER

There ain't much on the moon called Trask, other than endless oceans and a few black-market ports. But anyone who's touched down on that watery world has likely sampled the moon's famous chowder—a thick fishy soup (sometimes with rice, dependin' on the chef) made in large batches and dispensed into the bowls of hungry diners through ceiling-mounted hoses. This hearty dish was designed to warm up Trask's local fisherfolk after a long day at sea, so it's a natural addition to any midwinter celebration. What it lacks in appearance this chowder makes up for in taste. And if you're lucky, some bowls even come with an extra treat: a live cephalopod that adds an unexpected burst of flavor. If you've got any little ones 'round, though, you're probably gonna wanna make sure they stick to the broth and rice . . . just to be safe . . .

1 cup brown rice

1 tablespoon extra-virgin olive oil

8 ounces shiitake mushrooms, minced

1 medium onion, minced

2 garlic cloves, minced

2 teaspoons minced fresh ginger

2 tablespoons dried shrimp

6½ cups water

1 pound shrimp, peeled and deveined

1 tablespoon soy sauce

2 teaspoons sesame oil

¼ teaspoon white pepper

3 scallions, white and green parts diced, for garnishing

I can octopus in olive oil, for garnishing

> **PREP TIME:** 30 minutes
> **COOKING TIME:** 1 hour 25 minutes
> **YIELD:** 4 servings
> **DIFFICULTY:** Medium

1. Wash the rice, then transfer it to a medium bowl and cover with water. Soak for 30 minutes, then drain.

2. In a large pot over medium-high heat, heat the olive oil until it shimmers. Add the rice, mushrooms, onion, garlic, and ginger. Cook for 2 to 3 minutes, until softened.

3. Stir in the dried shrimp and water. Bring to a boil, then reduce the heat to low. Cover and simmer for 1 hour, stirring occasionally to prevent sticking. Add the fresh shrimp and continue to cook for 20 minutes, until thickened.

4. Stir in the soy sauce, sesame oil, and white pepper. Garnish with the scallions and octopus to serve.

Glazed Kod'yok

A few generations ago, kod'yok roamed the plains of the snowy world of Vandor in abundance. These shaggy beasts were great for ridin', but they were even better for eatin'. Locals knew how to use a kod'yok from tip to tail, turnin' their hide and fur into warm clothes while carvin' their delicious meat into a variety of prime cuts. But not everyone showed the kod'yok that level of respect. After the Empire occupied Vandor, the herds were dramatically thinned out, makin' kod'yok meat much harder to come by. What was once a staple for most folks on Vandor has now become a rare treat worth savin' for special events. And since there ain't no event more special than the holidays, seems like the perfect time to enjoy a hunk of kod'yok glazed in a traditional wroshyr sap syrup.

One 8-pound bone-in smoked ham, room temperature

¾ cup packed light brown sugar

¾ cup maple syrup

¼ cup pineapple juice

2 tablespoons Dijon mustard

½ teaspoon ground cinnamon

½ teaspoon black pepper

¼ teaspoon ground nutmeg

PREP TIME: 10 minutes

COOKING TIME: 2 hours

YIELD: 12 servings

DIFFICULTY: Easy

1. Preheat the oven to 325°F. Rinse the ham and pat dry. Place on a rack in a roasting pan. Use a knife to score diamonds into the surface of the ham. Set aside.

2. In a small bowl, whisk together the brown sugar, maple syrup, pineapple juice, mustard, cinnamon, black pepper, and nutmeg. Use a kitchen brush to apply this glaze on the ham, reserving half for basting.

3. Pour water into the bottom of the roasting pan. Cover ham with aluminum foil and bake for 2 hours, basting every 20 to 30 minutes, or until an instant-read thermometer registers 145°F when inserted into the thickest part of the ham.

4. Let rest for 20 minutes. Slice to serve.

EOPIE ROAST

There are lots of worlds where eopie is considered a delicacy. Personally, I never quite understood the appeal of gnawin' on tough meat from such an ill-tempered, flatulent creature. But a visit to Bakkar over at Ronto Roasters in Black Spire Outpost changed my tune. He lemme sample a slice of roasted eopie rump so tender that it practically melted in my big ol' mouth. The way his special seasonin' blend permeated the meat was pure magic. Bakkar ain't usually one to share his trade secrets, though, even with an ol' friend like me. Had to trade one of my best vibroknives to get the recipe from him, but I still think I came out on top in that deal. If you've got a special event on your horizon, holiday or otherwise, you can't go wrong with one of these roastin' in your oven.

5 garlic cloves, minced

3 tablespoons packed light brown sugar

1 teaspoon paprika

1 teaspoon salt

1 teaspoon black pepper

3 pounds pork loin

1 sprig fresh rosemary

PREP TIME: 5 minutes

COOKING TIME: 1 hour

YIELD: 6 servings

DIFFICULTY: Easy

1. Preheat the oven to 400°F. Prep a baking sheet with aluminum foil and set a wire rack greased with nonstick spray on top.

2. In a small bowl, stir together the garlic, brown sugar, paprika, salt, and black pepper. Rub the mixture on the pork loin. Transfer the pork, fat-side up, to the prepped wire rack and top with the rosemary.

3. Roast for 1 hour, or until an instant-read thermometer registers 145°F when inserted into the thickest part of the loin.

4. Let rest for 15 minutes. Slice to serve.

CRAIT CRUSTED COD

Tastes may vary wildly from one side of the galaxy to the other, but any decent chef on any world will agree that every good recipe shares one key ingredient: salt. And there ain't no salt as pure as the kind coverin' the surface of the planet Crait. I use that stuff in just about every dish I cook these days, but although it always does its job, salt rarely gets to be the star of the show. After years of bein' my silent partner in the kitchen, I finally decided to give this mighty mineral a chance to shine as bright as Crait's salt flats in the midday sun. By encasin' a whole fish in a thick crust of salt and bakin' it to perfection, you get not only a moist and tender meal but also a showstoppin' presentation that is ideal for any holiday table.

4 cups kosher salt

4 large egg whites, lightly beaten

¼ cup water

2 large lemons, sliced into rounds

2 pounds cod fillets

1 tablespoon extra-virgin olive oil

½ teaspoon paprika

¼ teaspoon black pepper

2 bunches fresh dill

4 sprigs fresh thyme

PREP TIME: 15 minutes

COOKING TIME: 25 minutes

YIELD: 4 servings

DIFFICULTY: Medium

Continued on next page . . .

1. Preheat the oven to 400°F.

2. In a large bowl, mix together the salt, egg whites, and water until the mixture resembles moist sand. Place half of the salt mixture on a rimmed baking sheet, patting it down to a ¼-inch thickness. Place half of the lemon slices on top of the salt.

3. Rub the fish with the olive oil and season both sides with the paprika and black pepper. Place the fish on top of the lemon slices. Cover the fish with the dill, thyme, and the remaining half of lemon slices, covering the fish completely. Use the rest of the salt mixture to encase the fish.

4. Bake for 25 minutes, or until an instant-read thermometer registers 140°F when inserted into the thickest part of the fillets.

5. Let rest for 5 minutes. Crack the salt crust. Remove the fish to serve.

MUSHBLOOM PIE

Although Wookiees are known for their impressive skill as hunters, turns out they ain't bad gatherers either. That's likely due to the fact that their homeworld, Kashyyyk, has plenty of luscious plant life for 'em to forage. Personally, one of my favorite ingredients found on the planet's forest floor is the mushbloom, a bulbous fungus the Wookiees consider a delicacy. But be careful! These bioluminescent beauties turn toxic when they reach maturity, so you gotta make sure to pick 'em early in their life cycle. If you can avoid gettin' poisoned by 'em, the mushbloom's meaty texture makes a solid substitute for meat on days when the hunt goes awry. My savory mushbloom pie also makes a great Life Day meal for those species who tend to be a bit more herbivorous than your average Wookiee.

MASHED POTATOES

3 medium russet potatoes, peeled and quartered

⅔ cup whole milk

4 tablespoons unsalted butter

1 teaspoon salt

¼ teaspoon white pepper

PREP TIME: 20 minutes

COOKING TIME: 55 minutes

YIELD: 6 servings

DIFFICULTY: Medium

FILLING

2 tablespoons extra-virgin olive oil

3 tablespoons unsalted butter, divided

2 medium carrots, peeled and diced

2 celery stalks, diced

1 medium onion, diced

8 ounces white mushrooms, sliced

8 ounces cremini mushrooms, quartered

2 garlic cloves, minced

1 tablespoon Worcestershire sauce

2 tablespoons tomato paste

1 teaspoon dried oregano

½ teaspoon paprika

½ teaspoon salt

¼ teaspoon black pepper

2 tablespoons grated Parmesan cheese

1. **TO MAKE THE MASHED POTATOES:** Place the potatoes in a large pot over high heat and cover them with water. Bring to a boil, then reduce the heat to low. Simmer for 12 minutes, or until tender. Drain, but do not rinse. Return the potatoes to the pot and mash them with the milk and butter. Season with the salt and white pepper. Set aside.

2. Preheat the oven to 375°F.

3. **TO MAKE THE FILLING:** In a large skillet over medium-high heat, heat the olive oil and 1 tablespoon butter until the oil shimmers. Add the carrots, celery, onion, white mushrooms, cremini mushrooms, and garlic, and cook for 5 to 6 minutes, or until softened. Stir in the Worcestershire sauce, tomato paste, oregano, paprika, salt, and black pepper. Cook for 2 to 3 minutes, until fragrant.

4. Pour the filling into a 9-by-9-inch baking dish. Evenly spread the mashed potatoes over the top, sprinkle with Parmesan cheese, and dot with the remaining 2 tablespoons butter. Place the dish on a baking sheet and bake for 30 minutes, or until browned and cooked through.

5. Let rest for 5 minutes before serving.

ROASTED ROOTLEAF

Nearly every planet from Dagobah to Dantooine has got some sort of creature that lives on it, but that don't mean every planet's got creatures worth eatin'! On some worlds, the options for quality meat are pretty slim, so you gotta find other ways to tempt your taste buds and fill your belly. That means usin' common ingredients in creative ways. Even somethin' as ordinary as a rootleaf can be transformed into a feast if you cook it up right. Few folks realize you can roast an entire head of the stuff and carve it just like a hunk of roast shaak. It's got all the potent flavor of my Rootleaf Stew recipe, and it's only about half as pungent! Sure, it might not be the most traditional entrée in your solstice spread, but honestly, who wouldn't be impressed seein' you carve up one of these on your special day?

1 head cabbage

1 medium onion, sliced

3 tablespoons packed light brown sugar

2 tablespoons extra-virgin olive oil

2 tablespoons orange juice

2 teaspoons dried mustard

1 teaspoon dried rosemary

1 teaspoon dried sage

1 teaspoon dried thyme

½ teaspoon garlic powder

½ teaspoon salt

¼ teaspoon black pepper

8 ounces white mushrooms, quartered

2 medium carrots, peeled and diced

2 cups vegetable broth, divided

PREP TIME: 10 minutes

COOKING TIME: 1 hour 30 minutes

YIELD: 6 servings

DIFFICULTY: Medium

1. Preheat the oven to 400°F.

2. Stem the cabbage to create a flat surface and cut off the top to open up the leaves. Use a paring knife to make small slits all over the cabbage.

3. Spread the onion evenly on the bottom of a Dutch oven. Place the cabbage in the middle.

4. In a small bowl, stir together the brown sugar, olive oil, orange juice, dried mustard, rosemary, sage, thyme, garlic powder, salt, and black pepper. Brush half of the spice mixture all over the cabbage, reserving the rest.

5. Add the mushrooms and carrots to the pot. Pour in 1 cup of broth. Cover the cabbage with aluminum foil and cook for 45 minutes.

6. Remove the foil and brush with the remaining spice mixture. Add the remaining 1 cup of broth to the pot, replace the foil, and cook for 45 minutes more.

7. Slice the cabbage to serve.

Barbecued Trakkrrrn Ribs

It ain't really a secret that Wookiees like to eat. Life Day may be the perfect excuse for 'em to indulge their appetites, but even when they aren't celebratin' somethin', those burly bipedals are commonly found chowin' down. And although they're usually more than glad to ingest whatever I put in front of 'em, I've never seen a Wookiee devour anythin' quite as fast as a rack of trakkrrrn ribs. Native to Kashyyyk, the trakkrrrn's meat has a natural spiciness that is brought to the surface when cooked low and slow. Serve a slab of these at your next gatherin', and you're bound to hear endless growls of joy. Your guests may leave you with nothin' but a pile of bones when the night is done, but at least it's not your job to clean the sauce out of their fur!

BARBECUE SAUCE

1 tablespoon extra-virgin olive oil

2 garlic cloves, minced

1 chipotle in adobo sauce, minced

½ cup ketchup

1 tablespoon sweet chili sauce

2 tablespoons packed light brown sugar

1 tablespoon apple cider vinegar

½ teaspoon ground cumin

½ teaspoon onion powder

½ teaspoon salt

¼ teaspoon black pepper

RIBS

4 pounds baby back pork ribs

2 tablespoons extra-virgin olive oil

¼ cup packed light brown sugar

2 teaspoons paprika

2 teaspoons salt

1 teaspoon garlic powder

1 teaspoon black pepper

PREP TIME: 10 minutes

COOKING TIME: 2 hours 30 minutes

YIELD: 4 servings

DIFFICULTY: Medium

1. Preheat the oven to 300°F. Prep a baking sheet with aluminum foil and place a wire rack on top.

2. **TO MAKE THE BARBECUE SAUCE:** In a medium saucepan over medium-low heat, add olive oil and garlic, cooking for 1 to 2 minutes, until softened. Stir in the chipotle in adobo, ketchup, sweet chili sauce, brown sugar, apple cider vinegar, cumin, onion powder, salt, and black pepper. Cook for 2 to 3 minutes, until fragrant. Let cool, then keep in the refrigerator until ready to use.

3. **TO MAKE THE RIBS:** Remove and discard the membrane from the ribs. Rub the ribs with the olive oil. In a medium bowl, stir together the brown sugar, paprika, salt, garlic powder, and black pepper. Rub the spice mixture on both sides of the ribs.

4. Place the ribs on the prepped wire rack and cover with foil, crimping the edges of the foil around the baking sheet to seal. Bake for 2½ hours, until tender. Remove from oven, open the foil, and brush the ribs with barbecue sauce. Set the broiler to high. Return the ribs to the oven and broil for 1 to 2 minutes, until sauce is caramelized.

5. Let rest for 10 minutes before serving.

KUBLAG CURRY

Few folks know how to throw an epic feast quite like the Ewoks. These adorable little fellas from the Sanctuary Moon of Endor may look like little bitty Wookiees, but it turns out that their appetites are equally as big. In the winter months, Ewoks have been known to hunt the six-legged kublag, usin' its meat to make a rich stew that can feed an entire village. They like to thicken the broth with raventhorn root and ground-apple stock, but my variation uses a unique spice blend I picked up from the Sakiyan food market on Tatooine awhile back. It's got a sweetness and warmth that could get you through even the coldest days. Pair it with a chunk of Rorkid Bread (page 41), and maybe a flask of sunberry wine from the chief's private stash, and you won't be able to resist joinin' the festivities.

CURRY BASE

⅓ cup yellow curry paste

One 14-ounce can chicken broth

2 whole garlic cloves, peeled

1 medium shallot, coarsely chopped

1 tablespoon packed light brown sugar

1 tablespoon extra-virgin olive oil

1½ teaspoons ground turmeric

1 teaspoon soy sauce

1 teaspoon Worcestershire sauce

1 teaspoon ground coriander

⅛ teaspoon black pepper

CURRY

2 tablespoons extra-virgin olive oil

1 medium onion, diced

1½ pounds boneless skinless chicken thighs, cubed

2 medium carrots, peeled and cut into rounds

2 medium russet potatoes, peeled and diced

One 14-ounce can full-fat coconut milk

1 cup water

Chopped fresh cilantro, for garnishing

½ cup store-bought crispy fried onions, for garnishing

1 Thai chile, sliced, for garnishing

1 lime, quartered, for serving

Cooked white rice, for serving

PREP TIME: 10 minutes

COOKING TIME: 35 minutes

YIELD: 6 servings

DIFFICULTY: Medium

1. **TO MAKE THE CURRY BASE:** In a blender, combine the curry paste, broth, garlic, shallot, brown sugar, olive oil, turmeric, soy sauce, Worcestershire sauce, coriander, and black pepper. Blend until smooth and set aside.

2. **TO MAKE THE CURRY:** In a Dutch oven over medium-high heat, heat the olive oil until it shimmers. Add the onion and cook for 2 to 3 minutes, until softened. Add the chicken and cook for 5 to 6 minutes, until browned. Stir in the curry base and cook for 3 to 4 minutes, until fragrant. Add the carrots, potatoes, coconut milk, and water. Reduce the heat to medium-low and simmer for 20 minutes, until vegetables are tender.

3. Garnish the curry with the cilantro, fried onions, and chile. Serve with lime wedges and rice.

ENGINE ROASTED TIP-YIP

Not everyone is lucky enough to be able to head home for the holidays. But those travelers who find themselves stuck spendin' Life Day on distant, unfamiliar worlds can still make the season bright by whippin' up this simple feast to enjoy with their crew. All it takes is a functionin' engine and a tip-yip—a common Endorian fowl that can be caught or bought on just about any world these days. See, tip-yip is absolutely mouthwaterin' when roasted at high temps . . . and there ain't no temp higher than the flames from a ship's thruster! The skin gets crispy, the meat stays juicy, and your crew will be singin' your praises (between verses of "Joh Blastoh"). You could also prepare this one in an oven, I guess . . . but where's the fun in that?

One 4-pound whole chicken

4 tablespoons unsalted butter, softened

4 garlic cloves, minced

2 teaspoons dried rosemary

1 tablespoon extra-virgin olive oil

1 tablespoon salt

1 teaspoon black pepper

1 medium lemon, halved

½ medium sweet onion

PREP TIME: 10 minutes

COOKING TIME: 1 hour 30 minutes

YIELD: 8 servings

DIFFICULTY: Medium

1. Preheat the oven to 425°F.

2. Remove and discard the neck and giblets from the chicken. Pat dry and loosen the skin. In a small bowl, stir together the butter, garlic, and rosemary. Rub the butter mixture under the skin, on the meat, and inside the cavity.

3. Rub the outside of the chicken with the olive oil. Season the outside and inside the cavity with the salt and black pepper. Place the lemon and onion inside the cavity. Tie the legs together with kitchen twine and tuck the wings under. Place on a rack in a roasting pan.

4. Roast for 1½ hours, or until an instant-read thermometer registers 165°F when inserted in the thickest part of the breast.

5. Tent the chicken with foil and let rest for 15 minutes. Discard the lemon and onion. Slice the chicken to serve.

BANTHA SURPRISE

Traditional holiday meals tend to be some of the most difficult to prepare. The more complicated a recipe gets, the harder it is to know when to stir, when to whip, or when to beat. Back when I was younger, I found a recipe for Bantha Surprise on an ol' holovid of my favorite chef, Gormaanda. No matter how many times I watched that vid, I could never get the dish to come out quite right. And to be honest, I'm not sure Gormaanda could either. So instead, I tried to capture the spirit of that holiday classic in my own variation, usin' veg and spices native to Kashyyyk to create a hearty and nourishin' Life Day feast. Bantha is pretty versatile, so you can always make this recipe your own, just like I did, by addin' ingredients native to your world.

MEAT

¼ cup all-purpose flour

1 teaspoon salt

1 teaspoon black pepper

2½ pounds boneless beef chuck, cubed

STEW

2 tablespoons extra-virgin olive oil

1 large onion, diced

2 garlic cloves, minced

One 32-ounce carton beef broth

1 cup red wine

1 tablespoon Worcestershire sauce

1 tablespoon tomato paste

1 tablespoon dried rosemary

1 tablespoon dried thyme

1 teaspoon paprika

½ teaspoon salt

½ teaspoon black pepper

1 bay leaf

3 medium carrots, peeled and cut into 1-inch pieces

2 celery stalks, cut into 1-inch pieces

1 pound small red potatoes, scrubbed

2 tablespoons cornstarch

2 tablespoons minced fresh parsley, for garnishing

> **PREP TIME:** 15 minutes
>
> **COOKING TIME:** 1 hour 45 minutes
>
> **YIELD:** 8 servings
>
> **DIFFICULTY:** Medium

1. **TO PREPARE THE MEAT:** In a shallow dish, combine the flour, salt, and black pepper. Dredge the beef in the flour mixture. Set aside.

2. **TO MAKE THE STEW:** In a Dutch oven over medium-high heat, heat the olive oil until it shimmers. Add the onion and garlic, and cook for 1 to 2 minutes, until softened. Add the dredged beef and cook for 3 to 4 minutes, until browned.

3. Stir in the broth, wine, Worcestershire sauce, tomato paste, rosemary, thyme, paprika, salt, black pepper, and bay leaf. Bring to a boil, then reduce the heat to low. Cover and simmer for 30 minutes. Add the carrots, celery, and potatoes. Cover and simmer for 1 hour, until vegetables are tender.

4. In a small bowl, make a slurry by combining the cornstarch and some stewing liquid. Pour the slurry back into the pot and simmer for 10 minutes, until the stew has thickened. Discard the bay leaf. Garnish with fresh parsley to serve.

DESSERTS

Let's be honest. As much as we all appreciate a well-crafted holiday meal, most of us are just clearin' our plates so that we can finally get to the best part of the menu: dessert. And if you happen to be searchin' for some of the galaxy's best confectionary creations, Life Day doesn't disappoint.

Even if you're like me and you already finish every ordinary meal with a sweet repast, there's somethin' undeniably special about holiday desserts. Maybe it's because they tend to come from recipes that've been passed down and refined over countless generations. Or it could just be the fact that you get to enjoy 'em with family and friends. Whatever the reason, every sugary bite tastes sweeter than ever 'round this time of year.

When I think about all of the traditional treats munched on in the midwinter months, it's kinda a wonder that I don't decide to skip the savory courses altogether. I mean, if I served a seasonal spread comprised of only cakes and cookies, I can't imagine anyone would complain.

If your dessert does happen to follow a full feast, be kind and give your guests a good glimpse of the decadence before they dig in to their dinners. That way, they can be sure to leave plenty of space in their stomachs.

Jelly Life Day Orbs

Although there ain't no doubt that Life Day's most iconic symbol is the Tree of Life, the glowin' orbs that the Wookiees use to decorate it are a close second. They might just look like big shiny balls of light to you and me, but each orb represents a specific memory in a Wookiee's family history. And since a Wookiee's lifespan is pretty long compared to most other species, a family can gather quite an impressive orb collection. They dangle most of 'em 'round their own tree homes, but each family picks out a favorite to hang in the Sacred Grove durin' Life Day's grand procession. Whether you've got a sentimental attachment to the orbs or not, though, there's no denyin' that their shimmerin' lights add somethin' special to the holiday. Create some new memories with this edible jellied version, a dessert that you and your loved ones ain't never gonna forget!

3 tablespoons superfine sugar

¾ teaspoon agar-agar powder

1½ cups water

¼ teaspoon edible luster dust

PREP TIME: 5 minutes, plus 4 hours to chill

COOKING TIME: 10 minutes

YIELD: 2 servings

DIFFICULTY: Easy

1. In a small saucepan over medium-high heat, whisk together the sugar and agar-agar powder with the water. Bring to a boil, then reduce the heat to low. Simmer for 2 minutes, until the mixture is clear. Let cool.

2. Pour the mixture into two spherical molds. Refrigerate for 4 hours.

3. Unmold the orbs onto a plate. Sprinkle with luster dust to serve.

SWEET ORGA ROOT PIE WITH ROASTED MICKELNUTS

We already know that Kashyyyk's sacred orga root is a Life Day staple, usually served right alongside the meal's main dish. But not many folks realize that the orga's natural sweetness makes it perfect for the dessert course as well. This orga root pie is not only a fun twist on tradition but also a guarantee that such an important ingredient won't get lost in the feast. To add a little crunch, I top this beauty with a smatterin' of roasted mickelnuts—an aromatic holiday favorite sold on the streets of Coruscant durin' Solstice Tide. A touch of dried wroshyr bark adds that extra hint of spice to bring it all together. It makes for an unforgettable dessert that gives the orga the respect it deserves in ways that your guests ain't likely to expect. But what are the holidays without a few surprises?

1 pound sweet potatoes, scrubbed

One 12-ounce can evaporated milk

¼ cup packed light brown sugar

¼ cup granulated sugar

2 large eggs, lightly beaten

1 large egg yolk

1 tablespoon maple syrup

1 teaspoon vanilla extract

¾ teaspoon ground cinnamon

¼ teaspoon salt

7 ounces store-bought pie dough

⅓ cup toasted pecans

2 cinnamon sticks, for garnishing

PREP TIME: 15 minutes

COOKING TIME: 2 hours 5 minutes

YIELD: 8 servings

DIFFICULTY: Medium

1. Preheat the oven to 375°F. Prep a baking sheet with parchment paper.

2. Pierce the sweet potatoes all over with a fork. Place on the prepped baking sheet and bake for 1 hour. Let cool.

3. Remove and discard the skin of the sweet potatoes, and place the sweet potatoes in a large bowl. Mash until smooth. Stir in the evaporated milk, brown sugar, granulated sugar, eggs, egg yolk, maple syrup, vanilla, ground cinnamon, and salt. Use a hand mixer to blend until smooth.

4. Grease a 9-inch pie plate with nonstick spray. Roll out the pie dough and press it into the pie plate. Prick with a fork and crimp the edges. Pour the sweet potato mixture into the pie crust.

5. Preheat the oven to 400°F. Place the pie plate on a baking sheet and bake for 15 minutes, then lower the heat to 350°F and bake for another 50 minutes, until set.

6. Let cool completely. Top with the pecans and garnish with cinnamon sticks to serve.

WASAKA BERRY PUDDING

A favorite among the Wookiees, this timeless steamed puddin' showcases a juicy berry gathered from the forest floors of Kashyyyk. Seems like somethin' that everyone could enjoy together on the holidays without much of a fuss, right? Not so much. See, nearly every Wookiee family has their own special recipe for this stuff, handed down across generations. They all believe that their version is the best, and for some reason, they're more than willin' to fight anyone who suggests otherwise. I tried a lotta different variations before settlin' on this recipe, which tries to capture the bright, tart flavors of the wasaka berry in a way that has universal appeal. Still, as mouthwaterin' as this one is, be careful who you serve it to. Just the slightest deviation could mean the difference between endin' your meal with a smile or without your arms!

1 cup raspberries

2 tablespoons honey

½ cup (1 stick) unsalted butter, softened

½ cup granulated sugar

2 large eggs, lightly beaten

2 tablespoons lemon zest

1½ teaspoons vanilla extract

1¼ cups all-purpose flour

5 tablespoons whole milk

½ teaspoon salt

1 cup raspberry jam

1 teaspoon lemon juice

PREP TIME: 15 minutes

COOKING TIME: 45 minutes

YIELD: 6 servings

DIFFICULTY: Hard

1. Grease a 7-inch springform pan with nonstick spray. In a small bowl, toss together the raspberries and honey. Spread the raspberry mixture evenly into the bottom of the prepped pan. Set aside.

2. In a large bowl with a hand mixer, cream the butter and sugar for about 4 to 5 minutes, until fluffy. Mix in the eggs, lemon zest, and vanilla. Mix in the flour, milk, and salt until just combined. Pour the batter on top of the berries.

3. Take a large piece of parchment paper and fold a pleat down the middle. Place on top of the pan and secure with kitchen twine.

4. Place a steamer trivet into the bottom of a large pot. Add water just up to the level of the trivet. Bring the water to a simmer over medium-high heat and place the pudding pan on top of the trivet. Place the lid on top. Steam for 45 minutes, adding more water as needed so the pot doesn't boil dry.

5. Carefully remove the pudding pan from the pot. Let cool slightly, then release the pan and invert the pudding onto a plate.

6. In a small saucepan over medium-low heat, heat the raspberry jam and lemon juice for 2 minutes, stirring constantly. Pour over the pudding to serve.

KLATOOINE CRÊPES

Goin' beyond your culinary comfort zone comes with the territory of bein' a chef. I've always done my best to keep an open mind—and an open mouth—when it comes to tryin' out somethin' new. Yet somehow, the Hutts make my edible explorations look basic and bland. See, the Hutts will eat just about anythin' you put in front of 'em. I've witnessed those gargantuan gangsters slurp down plenty of live meals, so it made me stop to ponder what they find so appealin' about 'em. In the case of the Klatooine paddy frog, it's the color and texture they adore. Fortunately, I was able to reproduce those qualities in a festive dessert that'll please just about anyone—no frogs required!

FILLING

½ cup unsweetened shredded coconut

½ cup packed light brown sugar

¼ cup full-fat coconut milk

CRÊPES

1 cup full-fat coconut milk

1 teaspoon pandan extract

2 large eggs

2 tablespoons unsalted butter, melted

1 cup all-purpose flour

½ teaspoon salt

> **PREP TIME:** 20 minutes, plus 1 hour to chill
>
> **COOKING TIME:** 25 minutes
>
> **YIELD:** 8 human servings, or one Hutt amuse-bouche
>
> **DIFFICULTY:** Hard

1. **TO MAKE THE FILLING:** In a medium saucepan over medium-low heat, stir together the coconut, brown sugar, and coconut milk, and cook for 10 to 15 minutes, until the ingredients are combined and slightly dry. Set aside to cool.

2. **TO MAKE THE CRÊPES:** Combine the coconut milk, pandan extract, eggs, butter, flour, and salt in a blender. Blend until just combined. Chill in the refrigerator for 1 hour.

3. Heat a medium nonstick skillet over medium heat. Add ¼ cup of crêpe batter, swirling until the batter coats the bottom of the skillet. Cook for 30 seconds, or until the edges are dry and the center is just set. Flip over and cook for another 15 seconds. Remove and set aside. Repeat with the rest of the crêpe batter.

4. Add 1 tablespoon of filling along the center of a crêpe. Fold the bottom over, then the sides, and finally the top. Serve seam-side down. Repeat with the rest of the crêpes and the filling.

MIRIAL TEACAKES

When it comes to the main course of any holiday banquet, you may have noticed that I tend to think big. The only real problem with servin' up a hearty hunk of meat and endless parade of sides is that there ain't much room left for dessert once folks are done. As much as I love to assemble a full fleet of sweet treats to follow any feast, I also understand the need to pull back on the throttle now and then. When somethin' a bit more delicate is called for in the final approach, I rely on these lovely little teacakes to bring the meal home. They may have gotten their name from the pink and green desert planet of Mirial, but don't worry—I promise they ain't nowhere near as dry! Make sure to bake a big batch, just in case your guests are hungrier than you thought.

1 cup cake flour

¾ cup granulated sugar

½ teaspoon baking powder

¼ teaspoon salt

4 ounces vanilla yogurt

¼ cup vegetable oil

½ teaspoon vanilla extract

3 large eggs, separated

¼ teaspoon cream of tartar

2 drops pink food gel dye

2 teaspoons matcha powder

1 tablespoon confectioners' sugar, for dusting

PREP TIME: 10 minutes

COOKING TIME: 20 minutes

YIELD: 12 servings

DIFFICULTY: Medium

1. Preheat the oven to 350°F. Prep a 12-cup cupcake pan with liners.

2. In a large bowl, whisk together the flour, sugar, baking powder, and salt. Make a well in the center of the flour mixture and stir in the yogurt, oil, vanilla, and egg yolks until combined.

3. In a separate bowl with a hand mixer, whip the egg whites and cream of tartar until stiff peaks form, about 4 to 5 minutes. Fold the whipped whites into the batter.

4. Separate the batter equally into two bowls. In one bowl, fold in the pink food gel dye. Fold the matcha powder into the second bowl.

5. Alternate the two batters by spoonfuls into the prepped liners, until three-fourths of the way full. Use a toothpick to make figure eights in the batter, until swirled.

6. Bake for 15 to 17 minutes, until a toothpick test comes out clean. Let cool on a wire rack. Dust with confectioners' sugar to serve.

WOOKIEE-OOKIEES

The more new worlds that start celebratin' a holiday, the easier it gets to lose track of where it all began. Honorin' the message of a day like Life Day is great, but we also gotta remember to pay respect to the celebration's origins. By alterin' the shape of these classic Kashyyykian cookies to look like tiny Wookiees, I aim to do just that. I was originally hopin' that a batch of these Wookiee-Ookiees could do double duty as both snacks and ornaments, but with their perfect balance of sugar and spice, they never ended up stayin' on the tree for long. So I came up with another recipe to use for decoratin', and saved this one just for savorin'. I'd never recommend bitin' a real Wookiee, but you're not gonna be able to resist chompin' down these sweet little fellas!

3 cups all-purpose flour

1 teaspoon baking powder

1 teaspoon ground cinnamon

¼ teaspoon ground nutmeg

¼ teaspoon salt

1 cup (2 sticks) unsalted butter, softened

½ cup packed light brown sugar

½ cup granulated sugar

1 large egg

2 tablespoons molasses

1 teaspoon vanilla extract

Black icing, for decorating

White icing, for decorating

PREP TIME: 10 minutes, plus 1 hour to chill

COOKING TIME: 10 minutes

YIELD: 12 servings

DIFFICULTY: Medium

1. In a medium bowl, whisk together the flour, baking powder, cinnamon, nutmeg, and salt. Set aside.

2. In the bowl of an electric mixer, cream the butter, brown sugar, and granulated sugar for about 5 to 6 minutes, until fluffy. Mix in the egg, molasses, and vanilla.

3. Add the flour mixture, mixing until the dough just comes together. Halve the dough and wrap each half in plastic wrap. Refrigerate for 1 hour.

4. Preheat the oven to 350°F. Prep two baking sheets with silicone baking mats or parchment paper.

5. Roll out the dough to a ¼-inch thickness. Use a gingerbread person-shape cutter to cut out shapes and transfer them to the prepped baking sheets. Use the back of a knife to create fur marks.

6. Bake for 10 minutes, then transfer the cookies to a wire rack to cool. Use the black and white icings to create face details. Let dry completely.

KASHYYYK CAKE

If you gave my previous batch of recipes a read, you'll probably remember the Wroshyr Tree Cake I used to bake for any Wookiees stuck celebratin' their special day at Maz's castle. I guess my furry friends could tell my heart was in the right place because it wasn't long before they started sharin' their own authentic Life Day recipes with me. Now that I've got an even stronger grasp on what Wookiees dine on durin' their sacred season, I've adapted my menu to reflect that in every course. These individual trifles, for instance, contain layered ingredients native to Kashyyyk, includin' the eggs of the wyyyschokk—an enormous spider-like creature that dwells in the planet's forests. Sure, this one don't look like a fancy tree, but I promise that it tastes exactly like Life Day should.

CHOCOLATE MASCARPONE

6 ounces mascarpone cheese

¾ cup confectioners' sugar

2 tablespoons cocoa powder

½ teaspoon vanilla extract

1 cup heavy cream

¼ teaspoon salt

½ cup (1 stick) unsalted butter

¾ cup granulated sugar

2 large eggs

1 teaspoon vanilla extract

¾ cup buttermilk

PREP TIME: 40 minutes

COOKING TIME: 20 minutes

YIELD: 6 servings

DIFFICULTY: Hard

CAKE

1½ cups cake flour

¼ cup cocoa powder

½ teaspoon baking powder

LAYERS

½ cup raspberry jam, divided

2 tablespoons chocolate pearls

1. **TO MAKE THE CHOCOLATE MASCARPONE:** In a medium bowl, stir together the mascarpone, confectioners' sugar, cocoa powder, and vanilla. Set aside.

2. In a separate medium bowl with a hand mixer, whip the heavy cream until stiff peaks form, about 6 to 7 minutes.

3. Fold the chocolate mascarpone mixture into the whipped cream. Keep in the refrigerator until ready to use.

4. Preheat the oven to 350°F. Prep a 9-by-13-inch baking pan with parchment paper and grease with nonstick spray. Set aside.

5. **TO MAKE THE CAKE:** In a large bowl, whisk together the cake flour, cocoa powder, baking powder, and salt. Set aside.

6. In the bowl of an electric mixer, cream the butter and sugar for about 5 to 6 minutes, until fluffy. Stir in the eggs and vanilla. Alternate adding the buttermilk and flour mixture until just combined.

7. **POUR THE BATTER EVENLY IN**to the prepped baking pan. Bake for 20 minutes. Let cool completely.

8. **TO MAKE THE LAYERS:** Cut the cake into cubes. Place half of the cake pieces into the bottom of 6 serving cups. Top each one evenly with half of the raspberry jam. Spoon on half of the chocolate mascarpone. Add the rest of the cake pieces and raspberry jam. Pipe the remaining mascarpone on top. Top with the chocolate pearls to serve.

Arayakyak Tarts

The fertile rainforests linin' the slopes of Mount Arayakyak have long been the source of many of Kashyyyk's most delicious fresh fruits. The Empire almost ended that when they laid waste to this region back durin' their occupation of the planet. But once those lousy moof-milkers were gone for good, nothin' could stop nature from takin' back over. You ask me, there ain't no better day to celebrate Kashyyyk's resilience and rebirth than Life Day. These tiny tarts pay homage to Arayakyak, made entirely from fruits and nuts that can be found growin' in the mountain's jungle orchards. For those who happen to be spendin' their Life Day on some other planet, though, there's no need to worry. You can easily sub in just about any berries local to your world with equally delicious results.

TOPPING

½ cup shelled raw pistachios

1½ tablespoons packed light brown sugar

1 tablespoon water

FILLING

⅔ cup granulated sugar

½ cup lemon juice

1 tablespoon lemon zest

2 large eggs

1 large egg yolk

5 tablespoons unsalted butter, cubed

⅛ teaspoon salt

CRUST

1 cup graham cracker crumbs

¼ cup chopped shelled raw pistachios

4 tablespoons unsalted butter, melted

1 tablespoon packed light brown sugar

⅛ teaspoon salt

4 raspberries, for garnish

¼ cup blueberries, for garnishing

4 fresh mint leaves, for garnishing

PREP TIME: 20 minutes, plus 30 minutes to chill

COOKING TIME: 20 minutes

YIELD: 4 servings

DIFFICULTY: Medium

1. **TO MAKE THE TOPPING:** In a small skillet over medium heat, stir together the pistachios, brown sugar, and water. Cook, stirring constantly, for 8 to 10 minutes, until sugar has dissolved. Spread the nut mixture evenly over a baking sheet lined with parchment paper. Let cool completely.

2. **TO MAKE THE FILLING:** In a double boiler over medium heat, whisk together the sugar, lemon juice, lemon zest, eggs, and egg yolk. One at a time, stir in the butter cubes, then stir in the salt, whisking constantly until thickened, about 10 minutes. Pass the curd through a fine-mesh sieve, then cover the surface with plastic wrap and chill until cold, about 30 minutes.

3. Preheat the oven to 350°F. Prep four small tart pans with nonstick spray.

4. **TO MAKE THE CRUST:** In a medium bowl, stir together the graham cracker crumbs, pistachios, butter, brown sugar, and salt until combined. Press the crust mixture evenly into each of the prepped tart pans. Bake for 10 minutes, until golden brown. Let the crusts cool completely.

5. Pour the curd into the prepped tart crusts. Decorate with the candied pistachio topping, raspberries, blueberries, and mint leaves to serve.

Jogan Fruit Parfait

No matter what planet you're dinin' on, there's a solid chance you'll be endin' your meal with a slice of jogan fruit cake. This sweet standard is enjoyed from Coruscant to Lothal, due in part to the fact that the round purple-and-white fruit that serves as the star of the recipe is grown on countless worlds. But although there's certainly a reason that folks across the galaxy love jogans, servin' somethin' so commonplace on a holiday just didn't feel right to me. But it also didn't make sense to leave a favorite out of the festivities, neither. So, I tried to capture the notes of the jogan in a whole new way, layerin' it with sweet creams and jellies in this cool and refreshin' parfait. Just like the holidays, this one reminds you of all the things you love while givin' you an entirely fresh perspective on what's possible.

GELATIN

2 envelopes unflavored gelatin

½ cup water

One 14-ounce can full-fat coconut milk

One 14-ounce can sweetened condensed milk

½ teaspoon ube extract

PARFAIT

1 pint ube ice cream

½ cup whipped cream

¼ cup sweetened coconut flakes

> **PREP TIME:** 30 minutes, plus overnight to set
>
> **YIELD:** 6 servings
>
> **DIFFICULTY:** Medium

1. **TO MAKE THE GELATIN:** In a small bowl, dissolve the gelatin in the water. Set aside. In a large saucepan over medium-low heat, bring the coconut milk to a simmer. Stir in the gelatin mixture. Remove from the heat. Stir in the sweetened condensed milk.

2. Separate the mixture evenly into two bowls. Leave one as is, and in the second bowl, stir in the ube extract. Pour the plain mixture into one 6-by-6-inch pan and the ube mixture into a second 6-by-6-inch pan. Place them in the refrigerator and chill overnight until set.

3. **TO MAKE THE PARFAIT:** Slice the gelatin into cubes and spoon into parfait glasses. Top with a scoop of ube ice cream, whipped cream, coconut flakes, and more gelatin to serve.

KABATHA CRISPS

While I was busy researchin' traditional Life Day fare, I also happened to stumble across a Kashyykian classic that I wanted to put my own spin on. Wookiees have a strange fondness for the guts of the kabatha, another species native to their homeworld. Kabatha is apparently considered part of a balanced breakfast on Kashyyyk, but although it may taste delightful, the texture leaves a whole lot to be desired—at least for folks of the non-Wookiee variety. If you ain't got fangs, it's tough to chew and hard to swallow. So, I decided to mix things up a bit, hopin' I could capture that signature kabatha flavor in a slightly more palatable form. After a few tries, I ended up with these fried Kabatha Crisps. Their sweet, airy layers make 'em a perfect treat for crunchin' on at any holiday gatherin'. Turns out, kabatha ain't just for breakfast anymore!

TOPPING

¾ cup granulated sugar

1 teaspoon ground cinnamon

DOUGH

3 cups all-purpose flour

3 tablespoons granulated sugar

1 teaspoon baking powder

½ teaspoon ground cinnamon

½ teaspoon salt

¾ cup Keshian Spiced Milk (page 100)

2 large eggs, lightly beaten

3 tablespoons unsalted butter, melted

1½ teaspoons vanilla extract

2 cups vegetable oil, for frying

PREP TIME: 20 minutes

COOKING TIME: 30 minutes

YIELD: 12 servings

DIFFICULTY: Medium

1. **TO MAKE THE TOPPING:** In a small bowl, stir together the sugar and cinnamon. Set aside.

2. **TO MAKE THE DOUGH:** In a large bowl, whisk together the flour, sugar, baking powder, cinnamon, and salt. Make a well in the center of the flour mixture. Stir in the milk, eggs, butter, and vanilla until just combined. Knead for 2 to 3 minutes, until the dough is smooth.

3. Divide the dough into 14 balls. Use a rolling pin to flatten them into thin 6-inch round discs. Let rest for 10 minutes.

4. In a Dutch oven, heat the oil to 365°F. Working in batches if necessary to avoid overcrowding, add the dough rounds and fry for 1 to 2 minutes on each side, until golden brown.

5. Remove the crisps and immediately toss them with the cinnamon-sugar mixture. Let drain on a wire rack before serving.

DRINKS

Libations may not be my primary area of expertise, but I've spent enough time in taverns and cantinas over the years to understand what it takes to quench someone's thirst. Sure, I'll always be more comfortable in front of a stove than behind a bar, but that ain't gonna stop me from pourin' a cup of good cheer for my guests on the holidays.

Whether you're lookin' to raise a toast or just kick back and relax, I'm certain I've got somethin' you can sip on. Some of these selections are classic midwinter beverages with a Life Day twist, while others are entirely new creations that I dreamed up from scratch. All of 'em made the list because their flavors managed to capture the spirit of the season in fluid form.

I know these potables aren't nearly as potent as the cocktails you can order at Oga's, but I can guarantee that they'll make you feel just as warm and cozy inside! That means you can treat yourself to a glass—or two or three—without any regrets. And if you ask me, that's the only way to spend the holidays.

WROSHYR SAP CIDER

By now, you're well aware of the wroshyr tree's deep significance to Life Day. But you may not realize that the Wookiee homeworld of Kashyyyk has over a thousand different varieties of the wroshyr fillin' its forests. Some might think the wroshyr's sticky, sugary sap seems the same from tree to tree, but I've noticed subtle variations in flavor dependin' on what type gets tapped. The slightly smaller trees found in the planet's coastal cities have a sweeter sap that's perfect for a glaze, while the sap of the colossal wroshyrs found in the planet's deep forests has a more robust profile that's ideal for sauces. But if you want a sap that's great for guzzlin', then the trees 'round Mount Arayakyak are the ones for you. The way their sap's fruity undertones bubble to the surface in this hot cider will have you wishin' that Life Day was every day!

6 cups unsweetened apple cider

2 tablespoons packed light brown sugar

3 cinnamon sticks

6 whole cloves

¼ teaspoon ground nutmeg

1 orange, sliced into rounds

6 orange peels, for garnish

6 cinnamon sticks, for garnishing

PREP TIME: 5 minutes

COOKING TIME: 10 minutes

YIELD: 6 servings

DIFFICULTY: Easy

1. In a large pot over medium heat, combine the apple cider, brown sugar, cinnamon sticks, cloves, and nutmeg. Place the orange slices on top. Simmer for 10 minutes. Strain the cider through a fine-mesh sieve and discard the cinnamon sticks and cloves.

2. Ladle the cider into mugs. Garnish with the orange peels and cinnamon sticks to serve.

BANTHA MILK HOT CHOCOLATE

Sometimes our journeys take turns that we never saw comin'. As a seasoned chef, I always believed my reputation would be tied to what I put on a plate, not what I poured into a glass. But after I released my first batch of recipes into the galaxy, my signature Bantha Chai quickly became one of my most-viewed creations on the holonet. Just like me, folks can't seem to resist the gentle aroma of the steamed bantha milk waftin' up from that warm mug. This new holiday variation keeps the familiar bantha blue but swaps out the tea for chocolate, addin' a richness that feels perfect for the season. I've got a feelin' I'll be pourin' my fair share of these over the midwinter months.

CREAM CHEESE TOPPING

4 ounces cream cheese, softened

¼ cup confectioners' sugar

¼ teaspoon salt

½ cup heavy cream

MILK

2 cups whole milk

½ teaspoon vanilla extract

3 ounces white chocolate, finely chopped

2 drops blue food gel dye

PREP TIME: 10 minutes

COOKING TIME: 5 minutes

YIELD: 2 servings

DIFFICULTY: Easy

1. **TO MAKE THE CREAM CHEESE TOPPING:** In a medium bowl, use a hand mixer to combine the cream cheese, confectioners' sugar, and salt. Add the heavy cream and whip until light and fluffy, 1 to 2 minutes. Keep in the refrigerator to chill.

2. **TO MAKE THE MILK:** In a medium saucepan over medium heat, heat the milk and vanilla for 4 to 5 minutes, until warmed. Stir in the white chocolate and blue food gel dye, whisking until combined.

3. Pour the mixture into two cups. Spoon the cream cheese topping on top to serve.

KESHIAN SPICED MILK

Runnin' a popular food freighter has its share of plusses and minuses. For example, whenever I bake a batch of Keshian Spice Rolls, they always sell out in an instant. Sounds great in theory, but it means I almost never get to pop one in my own mouth anymore. I'm left with nothin' but their aroma lingerin' in my kitchen, tauntin' me with their spicy sweetness all day long. That's why I brewed up this liquid version, featurin' some of the very same spices that make the rolls such a huge hit. The secret behind this flavorful beverage is that it's thickened with rice, providin' its smooth and creamy texture. But it's the variation of the Keshian spice blend, perfected by my late sous-chef, Robbs Ely, that really steals the show. This one will warm you up, body and soul. Just make sure to save a glass for yourself!

5 cups water

1 cup uncooked white long-grain white rice

3 to 4 cinnamon sticks

One 12-ounce can evaporated milk

½ cup granulated sugar

1 tablespoon vanilla extract

1 tablespoon ground cinnamon

PREP TIME: 15 minutes, plus overnight to soak

YIELD: 4 servings

DIFFICULTY: Medium

1. In a blender, combine the water and rice. Blend until the rice is finely ground, 2 to 3 minutes. Pour the rice water into a large bowl, then add the cinnamon sticks. Soak overnight in the refrigerator.

2. Strain the rice water through a fine-mesh sieve into a serving pitcher, discarding the rice and cinnamon sticks. Stir in the evaporated milk, sugar, and vanilla, stirring until the sugar has dissolved. Refrigerate until ready to serve.

3. Pour into glasses and dust with cinnamon, to serve.

Kyyyalstaad Fizz

There was a time not too long ago when it looked like the Wookiees might've celebrated their last Life Day. Imperial forces had occupied Kashyyyk, and the Wookiees were forced under their rule. The Empire did a lotta damage to the planet's ecosystem durin' their stay, tearin' down chunks of forests and buildin' processin' plants to exploit the world's abundant resources. But the tables eventually turned, and the Wookiees were able to seize back control of their world. Most of Kashyyyk's scars have long since healed, but some evidence of the Empire's reign still remains—includin' an abandoned refinery near Kyyyalstaad Falls that used to pollute the planet's pristine waters with its rancid runoff. Thankfully, those sparklin' cascades are crystal clear again and good enough to drink. So, in honor of Life Day—or whatever else you might be celebratin'—let's all fill our cups and raise a toast to a better tomorrow!

1 cup granulated sugar

1 cup water

2 cups cold sparkling water

1 cup lime juice

¼ cup lemon juice

1 cup ice, plus more for serving

1 lime, sliced into rounds, for garnish

Fresh mint, for garnishing

PREP TIME: 5 minutes
COOKING TIME: 3 minutes
YIELD: 8 servings
DIFFICULTY: Easy

1. In a medium saucepan over medium-high heat, cook the sugar and water for 2 to 3 minutes, until the sugar has dissolved. Let the simple syrup cool completely.

2. In a large pitcher, stir together the simple syrup, sparkling water, lime juice, lemon juice, and ice.

3. Pour the fizz into glasses filled with ice. Garnish with the lime slices and mint to serve.

SCARIF SLUSH

I first tried this unusual creation at a small resort on Scarif years ago—long before the Empire made a mess of the place with that blasted Death Star of theirs. The planet ain't much of a vacation destination anymore, what with its oceans boiled away and all, but I sure am glad someone managed to smuggle this recipe off-planet before the destruction ensued. With chilled chunks of tropical fruit swimmin' in a sweet milk-like liquid, this one probably falls somewhere between a refreshin' beverage and a fruit cocktail. Ultimately, what you've got yourself is an incomparable icy treat especially ideal for those celebratin' their holidays on any world with a warmer climate.

One 20-ounce can yellow jackfruit,
drained and sliced

½ cup young coconut,
drained and sliced

1 ripe avocado, peeled,
pitted, and sliced

½ cup full-fat coconut milk

¼ cup packed light brown sugar

4 cups finely shaved ice

¼ cup sweetened condensed milk

PREP TIME: 5 minutes

YIELD: 4 servings

DIFFICULTY: Easy

1. Spoon the jackfruit, young coconut, and avocado into four dishes. Pour the coconut milk on top, then sprinkle on the brown sugar. Spoon on the shaved ice.

2. Pour the condensed milk over each serving to serve.

SARJENN SNOWCAP

Some folks feel that frosty beverages in the colder months are as off-puttin' as a steamin' bowl of soup on a hot summer day. Personally, I happen to think there's somethin' kinda pleasant about bringin' your internal temperature down a bit closer to your external one. When I wanna embrace the chill of the season, I mix up this cold concoction, inspired by an icy astronomical object by the name of Sarjenn Prime. Ain't never been there myself, but I've heard secondhand stories of archaeological adventures on that frozen rock that pushed my imagination into overdrive. This drink mixes a sweet, slushy syrup with a swirl of cream for a chilly treat that's certainly worth explorin'. Add a stick of wroshyr bark if you want a bit of extra holiday flair!

Two 12-ounce cans cola

2 tablespoons sweetened condensed milk

2 cinnamon sticks, for garnish

PREP TIME: 15 minutes, plus overnight to freeze

YIELD: 2 servings

DIFFICULTY: Easy

1. Pour one can of cola into an ice cube tray and place in the freezer overnight.

2. Add cola ice cubes into the base of a blender. Pour in the second can of cola and blend until slushy.

3. Pour into two glasses. Top with condensed milk. Garnish with the cinnamon sticks to serve.

JOH BLASTOH PUNCH

As Life Day gets closer, folks start feelin' a touch more festive than usual. Once the orbs are hung, seasonal music begins to fill the streets of just about every spaceport marketplace across the Outer Rim. It's a great way to get travelers in the mood to shop for the holidays, but when you're stationed in one of those ports makin' meals for hours on end . . . well, let's just say the novelty eventually wears off. The other day, one of my sous-chefs told me that if she heard "Joh Blastoh"—a classic Huttese Life Day jingle—one more time, she was gonna punch someone. I managed to talk her down from turnin' to the dark side, but the conversation did inspire me to whip up this tasty Joh Blastoh Punch! It's got a rainbow of festive flavors floatin' in it, includin' a glob of signature Hutt green. Grab a glass and give your ears a rest, because this one is music to your mouth!

4 cups cranberry juice

2 cups pineapple juice

2 liters lemon-lime soda

½ gallon rainbow sherbet

PREP TIME: 10 minutes

YIELD: 16 servings

DIFFICULTY: Easy

1. In a large punch bowl, stir together the cranberry juice, pineapple juice, and lemon-lime soda.

2. Add scoops of the rainbow sherbet on top to serve.

"JOH BLASTOH"

The message of Life Day is still in the process of spreadin' its way across the galaxy. But even though some species may not be fully versed in the holiday's various traditions, there's a solid chance they can still hum along with a verse of one of Life Day's most famous songs. "Joh Blastoh" is a classic Huttese holiday jingle that's been covered by countless popular musicians over the years, from Luleo Primoc to Max Rebo. Rumor has it that R-3X—the DJ droid over at Oga's Cantina—has a collection of "Joh Blastoh" remixes so extensive that it could play all Life Day long without ever repeatin'. Sure, we may be destined to hear this tune ten thousand times in a single season, but once it starts playin', I dare you to try to resist singin' along.

Joh blastoh, joh blastoh
Blastoh moulee-rah
O ta panwa yataka
Bo eopie choppa

Jee bolla kyotopa hotu
Bo eopie choppa
Hari tish ding
Ho ho moulee-rah
Joh o tooka rundee
Koo rundee spira gusha
Haka panwa yataka tah
Choppa singee hunka be

Joh blastoh, joh blastoh
Blastoh moulee-rah
O ta panwa yataka
Bo eopie choppa

MUDHORN EGGNOG

On a visit to Arvala-7 awhile back, I was barterin' with some Jawas over a slightly used hyper-sonic oven when somethin' far more interestin' caught my eye. Although those pint-size pack rats usually deal in scavenged tech, they happened to be in possession of an item that was unmistakably organic—a big, furry egg unlike anythin' I had ever seen before. Turns out, it was from a local beast called a mudhorn, and the Jawas prized it as a rare delicacy. Never got that oven I came for, but I did manage to leave their sandcrawler with that egg. It cost me an entire cargo pod full of random appliances, but as soon as I cracked open its yolky center, I knew it was worth it. The egg became the perfect base for a thick, frothy batch of this nog, which kept me merry through an entire season.

2 cups whole milk

1 cup half-and-half

1½ teaspoons vanilla extract

1 cinnamon stick

½ teaspoon salt

4 large egg yolks

⅓ cup granulated sugar

4 large egg whites

1 tablespoon confectioners' sugar

½ teaspoon ground nutmeg

¼ teaspoon ground cinnamon

PREP TIME: 20 minutes, plus 30 minutes to chill
COOKING TIME: 15 minutes
YIELD: 6 to 8 servings
DIFFICULTY: Medium

1. In a double boiler over medium-high heat, heat the milk, half-and-half, vanilla, cinnamon stick, and salt. Bring to a simmer, 8 to 10 minutes.

2. In a blender, combine the egg yolks and sugar. Blend until light in color, about 1 minute. Temper the egg mixture by blending in ½ cup of the milk mixture, then slowly pour in the rest. Blend to combine.

3. Pour the blended mixture into a large saucepan. Cook over medium heat for 2 to 3 minutes, until just thickened. Let cool slightly, then transfer to a medium bowl and chill in the refrigerator until cold, about 30 minutes.

4. In a large bowl, beat the egg whites until soft peaks form, about 1 minute. Sprinkle in the confectioners' sugar, beating until stiff peaks form, about 4 to 5 minutes. Fold the egg whites into the cooled milk mixture until just combined.

5. Pour the eggnog into serving cups and sprinkle with the nutmeg and cinnamon to serve.

NOTE: This recipe contains raw egg. Because of the slight risk of salmonella, raw eggs should not be served to the very young, to the ill or elderly, or to pregnant women.

How to Celebrate Life Day at Home

This ain't easy for me to admit, but when it comes to throwin' a proper party, food is only part of the equation. If you really want folks to lose themselves in the merriment of the special day, then you gotta go above and beyond to set the scene.

Luckily, Life Day has its fair share of iconic ornamentation, from the red robes that Wookiees wear to the glowin' orbs they hang on their wroshyr trees. Unless you plan on visitin' Kashyyyk durin' the solstice season, though, gettin' your hands on authentic Life Day paraphernalia ain't always an easy option.

If you've got some extra credits janglin' in your pockets, I suppose you could pay to have the genuine artifacts delivered straight to your world. But much to the dismay of my favorite Ithorian importer, Dok-Ondar, I've always been the type who prefers to save some credits and come up with creative solutions of my own.

For those of you lookin' for some inspiration in your decoration, here's a collection of crafts that'll help you embrace the essence of Life Day without breakin' your budget. Put together some of these, and I guarantee that any Wookiee you happen to be hostin' will feel like they never left their tree house!

LIFE DAY ORBS

Did you know that the glowin' orbs the Wookiees display on Life Day were originally supposed to represent lumebugs? Accordin' to ancient legends, these luminescent insectoids swarmed from the Tree of Life when it was just a sapling, formin' all the stars in the sky. Not sure if there's any truth to the myth, but even if there ain't, it don't make the orbs any less lovely. I already gave you the recipe for some Jelly Life Day Orbs (page 77) that were designed to be a delicious and visually stunnin' part of your holiday spread. But if you're lookin' for somethin' a bit more traditional that you can actually hang on your holiday tree, you might wanna go with this crafted version instead.

YIELD: 12 orbs

Twine

12 clear glass ornaments

White glass paint

12 balloon lights

1. Tie the twine around the loops in the ornament caps.

2. Pour the glass paint into a paper bowl. Hold the ornaments by the top and dip them into the paint about one-third of the way up. Hang to let dry completely.

3. Once dry, remove the ornament caps and place a balloon light inside each ornament. Replace the caps and hang the ornaments on the tree to decorate.

TREE OF LIFE

As you're well aware by now, the Tree of Life is the most sacred symbol of Life Day. That means any Life Day celebration not featurin' some sort of fancy foliage instantly feels a lot less authentic. The forests of Kashyyyk may be filled with more sacred wroshyr trees than you can count, but not all worlds are quite so green. Sure, most planets have some sort of native flora they can use as symbolic substitutes, but folks who dwell in the deserts of Jakku or on the ice plains of Hoth have to be a touch more creative. That's where this handmade miniature Tree of Life (pictured on page 112) comes in. It may not be as majestic as the real deal, but it can survive on just about any world and still looks plenty nice to boot!

YIELD: 1 tree

1 roll brown craft paper

Floral wire

Scissors

Brown paint

Hot glue gun

½ pound green crinkle-cut shredded paper filler

1. Twist the craft paper into a 2-foot long tree trunk shape. Using the scissors, make 6- to 8-inch cuts in three places along the base to create the roots. Use floral wire to create branches and place them inside the trunk and roots as necessary to shape the tree. Add the brown paint to create bark details. Let dry.

2. Once dry, use the hot glue to adhere the crinkle-cut paper to create the greenery. Hang Wookiee-Ookiee Salt Dough Ornaments (page 119) and Life Day Orbs (page 115) to decorate.

LIFE DAY ROBES

The Wookiees I've encountered over the years rarely wear much more than the occasional bandolier. Most days, they don't seem to have a problem lettin' their fur flow freely in the breeze. But on a day as important as Life Day, I guess even Wookiees feel the need to get all gussied up. If you wanna look equally dignified, you can re-create their holiday look with these striking red robes. If you're plannin' on sharin' the love of the season with a variety of different species, though, don't forget to measure your guests appropriately. What may be the perfect length for you could be embarrassingly short for a Wookiee—or ridiculously long for an Ewok. In this galaxy, one size most definitely doesn't fit all!

YIELD: 1 robe

---

2 yards red fabric

Scissors

2 yards red ribbon, ends cut diagonally

---

1. Measure the fabric lengthwise to the desired length of the robe. Using the scissors, cut off the excess.

2. Lay the fabric flat. Along the top, fold the edge down 3 inches. On this fold, make a ½-inch cut every 2 inches to create a series of slits. Weave the ribbon in and out of the slits.

3. Drape the fabric over the shoulders and tie the ribbon to close.

WOOKIEE-OOKIEE SALT DOUGH ORNAMENTS

As I mentioned earlier, my adorable adaptation of the classic Kashyyykian Wookiee-Ookiees recipe (page 85) lets you bake up batches of cookies cute enough to display on any holiday tree. But the problem is, those sugary little Wookiees are so tasty that they tend to disappear before the party even gets started. In order to better separate the treats from the trimmins, I started makin' the Wookiee-Ookiees designated as ornaments out of a far more durable—and significantly less delectable—salt dough. Unlike their sweeter cousins, these salty fellas can last for years (as long as no one accidentally ingests 'em). If you happen to be makin' batches of both, be careful not to get the dough mixed up or your guests will be in for a holiday surprise they'll always remember . . . for all the wrong reasons!

YIELD: 10 ornaments

Medium bowl

Whisk

1 cup all-purpose flour

¾ cup ground cinnamon

½ cup salt

1 teaspoon ground nutmeg

1 teaspoon ground cloves

¾ cup warm water

Rolling pin

Parchment paper

Baking sheet

Gingerbread person-shape cookie cutter

Knife

Straw

Brown acrylic paint

Black acrylic paint

White acrylic paint

Ribbon

1. In a medium bowl, whisk together the flour, cinnamon, salt, nutmeg, and cloves. Stir in the water until the dough comes together, then knead for about 1 minute.

2. Preheat the oven to 200°F.

3. Use a rolling pin to roll out the dough between two pieces of parchment paper on a baking sheet to a ¼-inch thickness.

4. Remove the top piece of parchment paper and use the cookie cutter to cut out shapes. Remove the excess dough. Use the back of the knife to create fur marks. With the straw, make a hole at the top of the ornament. Reroll the leftover dough to make more shapes. Bake for 2½ hours, until dough is dry and hardened. Let cool on a wire rack.

5. Use brown acrylic paint to paint the ornaments. Once the paint is dry, use black-and-white acrylic paint to create face details. When dry, tie ribbons through the holes at the tops of the ornaments, then hang for decorating.

DIETARY CONSIDERATIONS

V = Vegetarian   GF = Gluten-free   V+ = Vegan

V*, V+* & GF* = Easily made vegetarian, vegan, or gluten-free with simple alterations.

APPETIZERS AND SNACKS

Shi-Shok Fruit Bowls GF V V+

Spiced Bogwings GF*

Bolus Nut GF V

Saava Snacks GF V V+*

Millaflower Toast V

Kebroot Parcels GF V V+

Yalbec Stingers GF V

Crab Puffs

Solstice Vegispheres V V+

Pickled Mynock GF

SIDE DISHES

Plicated Orga Root GF V

Spine Tree Spears GF V V+

Wroshyr Bramble V

Wawaatt Sprouts GF V V+

Rorkid Bread V V+*

Taba Leaf Salad GF V V+

Brub Berry Sauce GF V V+

Cirilian Noodle Salad GF* V V+

Gloomroot Pancakes GF* V

MAIN COURSES

Trask Chowder GF* V* V+*

Glazed Kod'yok GF

Eopie Roast GF

Crait Crusted Cod GF

Mushbloom Pie GF V

Roasted Rootleaf GF V V+

Barbecued Trakkrrrn Ribs GF

Kublag Curry GF*

Engine Roasted Tip-Yip GF

Bantha Surprise GF*

DESSERTS

Jelly Life Day Orbs GF V V+

Sweet Orga Root Pie With
      Roasted Mickelnuts V

Wasaka Berry Pudding V

Klatooine Crêpes V

Mirial Teacakes V

Wookiee-Ookiees V

Kashyyyk Cake V

Arayakyak Tarts V

Jogan Fruit Parfait GF V

Kabatha Crisps V

DRINKS

Wroshyr Sap Cider GF V V+

Bantha Milk Hot Chocolate GF V

Keshian Spiced Milk GF V

Kyyyalstaad Fizz GF V V+

Scarif Slush GF V

Sarjenn Snowcap GF V

Joh Blastoh Punch GF V

Mudhorn Eggnog GF V

Consuming raw or uncooked eggs may increase your risk of foodborne illness.

MEASUREMENT CONVERSION CHARTS

VOLUME

US	Metric
⅕ teaspoon (tsp)	1 ml
1 teaspoon (tsp)	5 ml
1 tablespoon (tbsp)	15 ml
1 fluid ounce (fl. oz.)	30 ml
⅕ cup	50 ml
¼ cup	60 ml
⅔ cup	80 ml
3.4 fluid ounces (fl. oz.)	100 ml
½ cup	120 ml
⅔ cup	160 ml
¾ cup	180 ml
1 cup	240 ml
1 pint (2 cups)	480 ml
1 quart (4 cups)	0.95 liter

TEMPERATURES

Fahrenheit	Celsius
200°	93.3°
212°	100°
250°	120°
275°	135°
300°	150°
325°	163°
350°	177°
400°	205°
425°	218°
450°	232°
475°	246°

WEIGHT

US	Metric
0.5 ounce (oz.)	14 grams (g)
1 ounce (oz.)	28 grams (g)
¼ pound (lb.)	113 grams (g)
⅓ pound (lb.)	151 grams (g)
½ pound (lb.)	227 grams (g)
1 pound (lb.)	454 grams (g)

About the Authors

JENN FUJIKAWA is the lifestyle and pop culture author of *Gudetama: The Official Cookbook: Recipes for Living a Lazy Life*, *The I Love Lucy Cookbook: Classic Recipes Inspired by the Iconic TV Show*, and *The Goldbergs Cookbook*. She has created content for Disney, Lucasfilm, Marvel, and more. As a contributing author to the official *Star Wars* website, she has created over 120 recipes on www.starwars.com. Unique family dinners and geeky baking are staples of her website www.justjennrecipes.com. She is based in Southern California.

MARC SUMERAK is an Eisner and Harvey Award–nominated writer whose work in a galaxy far, far away includes *Star Wars: Galaxy's Edge—The Official Black Spire Outpost Cookbook*, *Star Wars: Droidography*, *Star Wars: The Secrets of the Jedi*, and *Star Wars: The Secrets of the Sith*. Over the past two decades, his work has been featured in comics, books, and video games showcasing some of pop culture's most beloved franchises, including Marvel, Harry Potter, Firefly, Ghostbusters, Back to the Future, and many more. Find out more at www.sumerak.com. He is based in Cleveland, Ohio.

ACKNOWLEDGMENTS

This book is for the best droid builder in the galaxy—Grant Imahara, I miss you. Thank you to everyone who supported me when I needed it most. To my Wookiee family—my brother Mark Kawakami, whose AT-AT I coveted; my mom Alice Kawakami; and Kyle, Tyler, and Mason Fujikawa. To my Sarjenn System twin, Sarah Kuhn. To the best co-pilots in the galaxy, Mel Caylo and Chrissy Dinh. To the Galactic Senate with whom I can unconditionally talk with about *Star Wars*— Cheryl and Andre deCarvalho, Chrys Hasegawa, Robb Pearlman, Tina Pollock, Troy Benjamin, the GG; Andrea Letamendi, Christy Nett, and Amy Ratcliffe. To Peter Mayhew and Joonas Suotamo for bringing my favorite walking carpet to life. To my squadron leader Dan Brooks, for always giving me new challenges. To my own Jedi High Council—Harrison Tunggal for the great food conversations and support, and Marc Sumerak and Elena Craig for all the collaboration. And to the Maker, George Lucas, thank you for creating the vast universe that inspires me every day. —JENN FUJIKAWA

As Cookie says, "Life Day is about all of us." So thanks to the friends and fans across the galaxy who welcomed us into their special day, no matter what they may be celebrating. To the very best culinary crew this scruffy-looking nerf herder could ever hope for—Jenn Fujikawa, Elena Craig, and Harrison Tunggal. To Chelsea Monroe-Cassel and Chris Prince for setting the course on our first epicurean adventure. To Lucasfilm Publishing and Lucasfilm Story Group for their eternal wisdom and guidance. To Landry Q. Walker for giving Cookie his voice. To Scott Trowbridge, Margaret Kerrison, and the Galaxy's Edge team for bringing Cookie to Batuu. To George Mann and Cavan Scott for filling our midwinter months with mickelnuts and brub berries. To Jess, Charlie, and Lincoln for always keeping me on the path to the light. And, as always, to George Lucas for taking each and every one of us on this epic journey. Happy Life Day to all. May the Spires keep you! —MARC SUMERAK

INSIGHT EDITIONS

PO Box 3088
San Rafael, CA 94912
www.insighteditions.com

f Find us on Facebook: www.facebook.com/InsightEditions
🐦 Follow us on Twitter: @insighteditions

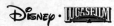

Library of Congress Cataloging-in-Publication Data available.

ISBN: 978-1-64722-477-6

Publisher: Raoul Goff
VP of Licensing and Partnerships: Vanessa Lopez
VP of Creative: Chrissy Kwasnik
VP of Manufacturing: Alix Nicholaeff
Editorial Director: Vicki Jaeger
Editor: Harrison Tunggal
Editorial Assistant: Maya Alpert
Senior Production Editor: Jennifer Bentham
Senior Production Manager: Greg Steffen
Senior Production Manager, Subsidiary Rights: Lina s Palma

Photography by Ted Thomas
Food and Prop Styling: Elena P Craig
Food and Prop Styling Assistant:
August Craig
Original art for pages 3, 6, 8–11, and 26 by
Joel Hustak

FOR LUCASFILM:

Senior Editor: Robert Simpson
Creative Director of Publishing:
Michael Siglain
Art Director: Troy Alders
Lucasfilm Story Group: Emily Shkoukani,
Kelsey Sharpe
Lucasfilm Art Department: Phil Szostak

ROOTS of PEACE   🌱 REPLANTED PAPER

Insight Editions, in association with Roots of Peace, will plant two trees for
each tree used in the manufacturing of this book. Roots of Peace is an inter-
nationally renowned humanitarian organization dedicated to eradicating land
mines worldwide and converting war-torn lands into productive farms and
wildlife habitats. Roots of Peace will plant two million fruit and nut trees in
Afghanistan and provide farmers there with the skills and support necessary
for sustainable land use.

Manufactured in China by Insight Editions

10 9 8 7 6 5 4 3 2 1